INSTRUCTOR'S MANUAL

AND

TEST BANK

to accompany

CULTURAL ANTHROPOLOGY, 5th Edition

prepared by **James E. Myers** *California State University, Chico*

Holt, Rinehart and Winston

New York   Chicago   San Francisco   Philadelphia
Montreal   Toronto   London   Sydney   Tokyo
Mexico City   Rio de Janeiro   Madrid

ISBN 0-03-006037-0

CBS COLLEGE PUBLISHING
Holt, Rinehart and Winston
The Dryden Press
Saunders College Publishing

TABLE OF CONTENTS

INTRODUCTION

USING THE INSTRUCTOR'S MANUAL

This Instructor's Manual is designed to accompany <u>Cultural Anthropology</u>, Fifth Edition, by William A. Haviland. Its objective is to provide intructors an extensive resource base to draw from in order to make the text more useful to them and to make the course more satisfying to the student.

The Manual has been divided into five sections:

1. INTRODUCTION
   Using the Instructor's Manual
   Integrating the Instructor's Manual with the Text

2. GENERAL RESOURCES AND REFERENCES
   Course Resources for Teaching Cultural Anthropology
   Field Projects/Class Activities
   Readers for Introductory Cultural Anthropology in Paper-
      back Editions
   Ethnographies
      Ethnographic Series in Paperback Editions
      Narrative Accounts of Fieldwork and Ethnographic Novels
         in Paperback Editions
   Monographs in Paperback Editions to Accompany the Text

3. FILMS
   Faces of Culture
   General References
   Media Resource Centers
   Film Distributors

4. CHAPTER GUIDES
   Supplementary Notes and Objectives
   Class Activities/Applications
   Film Suggestions

5. TEST BANK

It may be helpful to you to examine the individual components in Part 4, the Chapter Guides. Each Guide has been divided into three sections: Supplementary Notes and Objectives, Class Activities/Applications, and Film Suggestions.

Supplementary Notes and Objectives

This section is designed to call attention to a main feature of the chapter, or to give an additional thought that would be useful as a catalyst for class discussion.

The learning objectives that follow each section of Supplementary Notes are intended to help you determine what each student should have learned after reading the chapter.

Class Activities/Applications

This section provides a combination of things to do in class to stimulate discussion or projects that can be assigned that require the student to move out of the classroom into the campus or the community.

Film Suggestions

An annotated list of films to use with each chapter of the Haviland text is also included in the Instructor's Manual. Over 100 films are listed and annotated, each helpful when it comes to illustrating a culture or concept. The films can also be used to stimulate discussion or to develop analytical skills among the students. An index of Film Distributors is listed on pages xxv and xxvi.

Integrating the Instructor's Manual with the Text

The General Resources and References section provides the instructor with a large variety of suggestions and supplementary materials that can be used with the text.

For example, under the Field Projects/Class Activities section, Crane and Angrosino, Field Projects in Anthropology, provides exercises and field projects the student may undertake in order to gain greater depth of understanding of the participant-observation technique in ethnography.

Under Ethnographies, two helpful lists included are: a) highly readable narrative accounts of anthropologists' fieldwork experiences and ethnographic novels, and b) readable monographs in paperback editions. The narrative accounts and novels may provide students with greatly increased insight into the functioning of cultures from the natives' viewpoints as well as illustrate graphically the tremendous diversity of human cultural adaptations. Several of these works may be selected for supplementary readings. The monographs provide full ethnographic background to many of the cultures, past and present, that are discussed and used as examples in the Haviland text.

It is hoped that this manual will give instructors an extensive resource base from which to draw in order to make the text even more useful to them and to make the course even more satisfying to the student.

GENERAL RESOURCES AND REFERENCES

Course Resources for Teaching Cultural Anthropology

1. Attenborough, David. The Tribal Eye. New York: W. W. Norton, 1977. This book is based on the BBC Television series of the same name. It is a dramatic account of the film crew's experiences in the various places where they shot the series. The text is fascinating, revealing much background information that supplements the films very well. If the Tribal Eye films are used in the course, then this book is must reading.

2. Bernard, H. Russell and W. E. Sibley. Anthropology and Jobs: A Guide for Undergraduates. Washington, DC: American Anthropological Association, 1975. A helpful aid in answering questions about the kinds of jobs that are available outside of college teaching.

3. Clark, Grahame. World Prehistory in a New Perspective. New York: Cambridge University Press, 1977. Well-illustrated introduction to prehistory. Works well with chapter 3, The Beginnings of Human Culture.

4. Council on Anthropology and Education Quarterly. Available through the American Anthropological Association, 1703 New Hampshire Avenue, N.W., Washington, D. C., 20009. Frequently has articles devoted to the teaching of anthropology at all levels. Also often provides innovative ideas and course outlines for the classroom.

5. Edgerton, Robert B. and L. L. Langness. Methods and Styles in the Study of Culture. San Francisco: Chandler and Sharp, 1974. A concise, readable overview of the major methodological approaches used in ethnography and ethnology.

6. Fried, Morton H. The Study of Anthropology. New York: Thomas Y. Crowell, 1974. Discusses the history of the field, introductory courses, library materials, available occupations for a career in the field, consideration of

the question of ethics and research, etc. As valuable to the student as it is to the teacher.

7. Harris, Marvin. The Rise of Anthropological Theory. New York: Thomas Y. Crowell, 1968. Excellent overview of the entire history of theory development in anthropology. Only drawback, if it is one, is portrayal of cultural ecology as the theory by which all others should be judged.

8. Langness, L. L. The Study of Culture. San Francisco: Chandler and Sharp, 1974. Provides a concise review in readable form of the major aspects of the theoretical developments in cultural anthropology.

9. Mandelbaum, David G., Gabriel W. Lasker, and Ethel M. Albert, eds. The Teaching of Anthropology. Abridged edition. Berkeley: University of California Press, 1967. This paperback edition of the original massive work is well worth reviewing for its suggestions for organizing courses in the following areas: general anthropology, physical anthropology, cultural anthropology, archeology, linguistics, and applied anthropology.

10. Martin, M. Kay and Barbara Voorhies. Female of the Species. New York: Columbia University Press, 1975. Provides a systematic, cross-cultural overview of the role females have played and play in human societies. Useful book on this topic. Could be used as a text supplement.

11. McKeachie, Wilbert J. Teaching Tips: A Guidebook for the Beginning College Teacher, Sixth Edition. Lexington, Mass.: D. C. Heath and Company, 1969. Informative handbook for any college teacher. Although a general reference work, has many useful suggestions about preparing for a course, writing an outline, meeting class for the first time, lecturing, labs, media techniques, role playing, term papers, exams, grading, and so forth.

12. Pfeiffer, John E. The Emergence of Society: A Prehistory of the Establishment. New York: McGraw-Hill, 1977. Very readable work that outlines the development of civilizations in all the major areas of the world. It is unique in that Pfeiffer has gathered some data that has not yet even been published.

13. Sharer, R. J. and Wendy Ashmore. Fundamentals of Archaeology. Menlo Park: Benjamin/Cummings Publishing Company, 1980. Another well-written book. Provides much useful information about archeological methods and processes. Probably the best summary available on this topic.

14. Tanner, Nancy. On Becoming Human. New York: Cambridge University Press, 1981. Excellent supplement to the Haviland text.

15. Voget, Fred W. A History of Ethnology. New York: Holt, Rinehart and Winston, 1975. An important reference work on the topic that supplements Harris' classic work cited above.

Field Projects/Class Activities

1. Agar, Michael H. The Professional Stranger: An Informal Introduction to Ethnography. New York: Academic Press, 1980. This book introduces an ethnographic perspective to the study of human life. While not intended as a methodological cookbook, several problems in ethnographic interviewing and observation are discussed. An excellent source to help students conduct some of the class activities and applications suggested in each section of this Instructor's Manual.

2. Crane, Julia G. and Michael V. Angrosino. Field Projects in Anthropology: A Student Handbook. Morristown, N. J.: General Learning Press, 1974. Provides the undergraduate student with many helpful suggestions and hints about practicing anthropology in the field. Includes information on mapmaking, charting kinship, interviewing, collecting life histories, folklore analysis, ethnosemantic research, standardized questionnaires, photography, and planning a community study.

3. Hunter, David B. and MaryAnn B. Foley. Doing Anthropology: A Student-Centered Approach to Cultural Anthropology. New York: Harper & Row, 1976. In a "how-to-do-it" format, the authors provide information and exercises that teach students how to think and observe as anthropologists would. With its total methodological emphasis, would supplement the text well.

4. Ives, Edward. The Tape-Recorded Interview: A Manual for Fieldworkers. Knoxville: University of Tennessee Press, 1980. Excellent source for anyone planning on tape-recording an interview.

5. Lawless, Robert, V. Sutlive, and M. Zamora, eds. Fieldwork: The Human Experience. New York: Gordon and Breach Science Publishers, 1983. This reader includes articles by American and Third World anthropologists on the fieldwork experience. Each chapter offers a unique perspective on the important issues of fieldworker identity and its development in traditional and modern fieldwork.

6. Pelto, Pertti J. <u>Anthropological Research: The Structure of Inquiry</u>. New York: Harper and Row, 1970. Comprehensive methodological summary of field methods and methods of analysis used in ethnology.

7. Spradley, James. <u>The Ethnographic Interview</u>. New York: Holt, Rinehart, and Winston, 1979. Excellent primer for the neophyte ethnographer.

8. Spradley, James P. and David W. McCurdy. <u>The Cultural Experience: Ethnography in Complex Society</u>. Chicago: Science Research Associates, 1972. Gives students some ideas on how to formulate research problems and carry them out within their own cultural context. Five theoretical chapters are followed by twelve small "field" projects during the course.

Readers for Introductory Cultural Anthropology in Paperback Editions

1. Alger, Norman, ed. <u>Many Answers: A Reader in Cultural Anthropology</u>. St. Paul: West, 1974. The editor selected the articles to provide a view of the range of human behavior and to include only those that were readable and appealing to students. The result is a mixture of some good, some mediocre, articles that fit the text only with some difficulty, but it is worth investigating.

2. Annual Editions, <u>Readings in Anthropology 85/86</u>. Guilford, CT: The Dushkin Publishing Group, 1985. Brings together many exciting and highly readable articles, most of recent publication. Although the arrangement would not easily fit the structure of the Haviland text, the articles can be assigned individually without much problem.

3. Arens, W. and Susan Montague, eds. <u>The American Dimension: Cultural Myths and Social Realities</u>, Second Edition. Port Washington, NY: Alfred Publishing Co., 1981. A collection of light articles using symbolic content analysis to describe aspects of American culture. <u>Star</u>, <u>The Exorcist</u>, and astrology, for example, all come under the lamp for inspection.

4. Bernard, H. Russell, ed. <u>The Human Way: Readings in Anthropology</u>. New York: Macmillan, 1975. A truly readable and instructive set of readings that would be an excellent accompaniment for the Haviland text.

5. Cohen, Yehudi A., ed. <u>Man in Adaptation: The Cultural Present</u>, Second Edition. Chicago: Aldine, 1974. Stateless Societies (subdivided into Hunting-gathering and Pastoral) and State Societies (subdivided into Cultivating and Industrial). Takes a straightforward approach to providing

the social-political-economic background of human societies.

6. Cohen, Yehudi A., ed. Man in Adaptation: The Institutional Framework. Chicago: Aldine, 1971. Considers the topics of: Marriage and the Family, Law and Social Control, Religion and Magic, Values and Ideology, Personality, and the Arts. Serious straightforward collection of articles in a topic outline. Worth considering as an accompaniment to the Haviland text.

7. Cole, Johnetta B., ed. Anthropology for the Eighties: Introductory Readings. New York: The Free Press, 1982. Although designed by the editor to serve as the principal book for an introductory cultural course, the thirty-two articles would be worthwhile as supplementary readings to the Haviland text.

8. Goldschmidt, Walter. Exploring the Ways of Mankind: A Text-Casebook, 3rd edition. New York: Holt, Rinehart and Winston, 1977. A very successful reader of fifty-eight articles that can be easily integrated with Haviland.

9. Gould, Richard A. and the editors of Natural History magazine. Man's Many Ways, Second Edition. New York: Harper & Row, 1977. Approximately twenty-five short articles by anthropologists that have appeared in Natural History magazine, some of which are excellent.

10. Hammel, Eugene A. and William S. Simmons, eds. Man Makes Sense: A Reader in Cultural Anthropology. Boston: Little, Brown, 1970. Twenty-five articles, some of which are original, divided into two major themes: the personality of anthropology and structure, time, and symbols. Important articles, but not always easy for the beginning student.

11. Hammond, Peter B., ed. Cultural and Social Anthropology: Introductory Readings in Ethnology, Second Edition. New York: Macmillan, 1975. Good selection of articles, topically arranged. Would fit the Haviland text fairly well.

12. Hughes, Charles C., ed. Custom Made: Introductory Readings for Cultural Anthropology, Second Edition. Chicago: Rand McNally, 1976. Approximately fifty short articles from well-known authors organized around the central concept of culture. Would not fit easily with the Haviland text, but the articles are quite good.

13. Hunter, David E. and Phillip Whitten, eds. Anthropology: Contemporary Perspectives. Second Edition, 1982, Boston: Little, Brown, 1982. Exciting, readable, short articles on general anthropology. There are forty-six articles drawn

from a great variety of sources. Unfortunately, structure would not easily fit the Haviland text.

14. Jennings, Jesse D. and E. Adamson Hoebel, eds. <u>Readings in Anthropology</u>, Third Edition. New York: McGraw-Hill, 1972. A reader to accompany a general text; many articles are classics in the field. Some would fit quite well with the Haviland text.

15. Jorgensen, Joseph G. and Marcell Truzzi, eds. <u>Anthropology and American Life</u>. Englewood Cliffs, NJ: Prentice-Hall, 1974. Interesting collection of introductory cultural anthropology articles using American society as the ethnographic source. If you are interested in this book, also see Spradley, <u>Nacerima</u>, and Arens and Montagu, <u>The American Dimension</u>, in this listing.

16. Langness, L. L. <u>Other Fields, Other Grasshoppers: Readings in Cultural Anthropology</u>. New York: J. B. Lippincott Co., 1977. A superb collection of essays designed to help the student examine human diversity and the dignity of human life wherever it is found. Worth the effort required to fit the readings into the Haviland text structure.

17. McCurdey, David W. and James Spradley. <u>Issues in Cultural Anthropology: Selected Readings</u>. Boston: Little, Brown and Co., 1979. An excellent collection of readings involving issues that have concerned but often divided anthropologists.

18. Poggie, John J., Jr., Gretel H. Pelto, and Pertti Pelto, eds. <u>The Evolution of Human Adaptations: Readings in Anthropology</u>. New York: Macmillan, 1976. Excellent collection of articles topically arranged. With some juggling, it would fit well with Haviland text.

19. Rosaldo, Michelle Zimbalist and Louise Lamphere, eds. <u>Women, Culture and Society</u>. Stanford: Stanford University Press, 1974. Excellent selection of articles on the topic that could be used to supplement the text and other readings.

20. Rossi, Ino, J. Buettner-Janusch, and D. Coppenhaver, <u>Anthropology Full Circle</u>. New York: Praeger, 1977. Sixty-three articles covering the four major fields of anthropology: physical, cultural, archeology, and linguistics. Another good book of readings to accompany Haviland.

21. Spradley, James P. and David W. McCurdy, eds. <u>Conformity and Conflict: Readings in Cultural Anthropology</u>, Fourth Edition. Boston: Little, Brown, 1980. A much-revised,

popular anthology, with many excellent selections which could be related to the Haviland text. Has a strong culturalist perspective and neglects much of the ecological perspective.

22. Spradley, James P. and Michael A. Rynkiewich, eds. The Nacerima: Readings on American Culture. Boston: Little, Brown, 1975. Another excellent collection of articles on American culture to illustrate introductory concepts in cultural anthropology.

23. Tax, Sol and Leslie G. Freeman, eds. Horizons of Anthropology, Second Edition. Chicago: Aldine, 1977. Expanded and updated edition of earlier work that summarizes the state of anthropology in all the major fields. It could easily be used with the Haviland text. Authors of the articles are all noted anthropologists, experts in their fields.

24. Weaver, Thomas, general ed. To See Ourselves: Anthropology and Modern Issues. Approximately 50 articles by noted anthropologists and sociologists dealing with contemporary social problems and issues. Could not be easily adapted to the Haviland text, but would be an excellent source for stimulating discussion on a variety of crucial social issues for the United States, the world, and anthropologists.

Ethnographies

Ethnographic Series in Paperback Editions

1. Spindler, G. and L. Spindler, general eds. Case Studies in Cultural Anthropology. New York: Holt, Rinehart and Winston. Approximately 90 titles averaging 100 pages each. There is a title for almost any type of culture in almost any part of the world.

2. Spindler, G. and L. Spindler, general eds. Case Studies in Education and Culture. New York: Holt, Rinehart and Winston. Approximately 17 titles averaging 100 pages each. Emphasizes cross-cultural practices on enculturation, formal and informal. Brief ethnographic synopsis at the beginning precedes each text.

Narrative Accounts of Fieldwork and Ethnographic Novel in Paperback Editions

1. Achebe, Achinua. Things Fall Apart. New York: Fawcett World, 1969. Excellent novel that can be suited to any introductory course. As with writings of this genre, it provides the student with an intimate insider's view of another culture. It is especially noteworthy for the theme of social change that is brought about by British

colonization of Nigeria and the effects of the introduction of Christianity on the Ibo people.

2. Alland, Alexander, Jr. When the Spider Danced: Notes from an African Village. Garden City, NY: Doubleday, 1975. Entertaining, fascinating narrative account of a well-known anthropologist's first field experience. The setting is the Ivory Coast where Alland worked with the Abron people.

3. Berreman, Gerald D. Behind Many Masks: Ethnography and Impression Management in a Himalayan Village. Society for Applied Anthropology, Monograph No. 4, 1962. Also available as a Bobbs-Merrill Reprint. Excellent, brief account of the author's fieldwork in an Indian community. Narrative is followed by analysis based on Goffman's impression management model.

4. Biocca, Ettore. Yanomamo: Narrative of a White Girl Kidnapped by Amazonian Indians, as Told to Ettore Biocca. New York: E. P. Dutton, 1970. Fascinating account that would supplement Chagnon's work among the Yanomamo.

5. Bowen, Elenore Smith. Return to Laughter. Garden City, NY: Doubleday, 1954. Anthropologist Laura Bohannan's famous work about her trials and tribulations doing fieldwork among the horticultural Tiv of Nigeria. Highly recommended by all who have read it.

6. Briggs, Jean L. Never in Anger: Portrait of an Eskimo Family. Cambridge, MA: Harvard University Press, 1970. Another excellent and oft-assigned work providing an account of this anthropologist's work among the Utkuhik-halingmiut Eskimo northwest of Hudson Bay. Would fit well with the Haviland text.

7. Fernea, Elizabeth. Guests of the Sheik: An Ethnography of an Iraqi Village. New York: Doubleday Anchor, 1965.

8. Fernea, Elizabeth Warnock. A Street in Marrakech. Garden City, NY: Doubleday, 1976. The dust jacket describes it as "a personal encounter with the lives of Moroccan women."

9. Icaza, Jorge. The Villagers (Huasipungo). Carbondale and Edwardsville, IL: Southern Illinois University Press, 1964. (Originally published in Spanish in 1934.) Powerful novel by Ecuadorean author Icaza that describes a hacienda in highland Ecuador and the lives of the peasants (huasipungueros) that work on it. The tragic but heroic ending of the novel says much about traditional peasant life.

10. Jesus, Carolina Marie de. Child of the Dark: The Diary of Maria Carolina de Jesus. New York: E. P. Dutton, 1962.

True story of a woman living in the favelas (slums) of Sao Paulo, Brazil. Would fit well with the last three chapters of Haviland.

11. Lamb, F. Bruce. Wizard of the Upper Amazon: The Story of Manuel Cordova-Rios. Boston: Houghton Mifflin, 1975. Fascinating story of a Peruvian rubber tapper captured and groomed to become the chief of a group of Amahuaca Indians in the Peruvian Amazon region. Particularly noteworthy for the role of the hallucinogen ayauasca (Banisteriop iscaapi) in hunting ceremonies.

12. Lewis, Oscar. Five Families. New York: Basic Books, 1959. One of Lewis' classic works, describes five Mexican families which represent differing stages of acculturation and urbanization.

13. Lewis, Oscar. The Children of Sanchez. New York: Random House, 1961. Another classic work by the author that describes in detail the life of a poor Mexican family living in Mexico City.

14. Maybury-Lewis, David. The Savage and the Innocent. Boston: Beacon, 1965. Very interesting narrative account of the author's fieldwork experiences among the Akwe-Shavante of Central Brazil. Reads like a novel.

15. Mintz, Sidney W. Worker in the Cane: A Puerto Rican Life History. New York: W. W. Norton, 1974 (originally published in 1960). Well-written, interesting account that could be used in place of Oscar Lewis' work on Puerto Rican life, La Vida, which is probably too long to be used in an introductory course.

16. Neihardt, John G. Black Elk Speaks. New York: Simon and Schuster, 1972 (originally published in 1959). Black Elk was an Oglala Sioux medicine man who lived through the period of the Ghost Dance religion in the U.S. This book is his biography. Excellent reading to illustrate shamanism and revitalization movements.

17. Pozas, Ricardo. Juan the Chamula: An Ethnological Recreation of the Life of a Mexican Indian. Translated from the Spanish. Berkeley: Unviversity of California Press, 1971. Short novel of a Chamula Indian who rejects acculturation. Also related to theme of culture change and religion. Well-written, but needs explanation.

18. Powdermaker, Hortense. Stranger and Friend: The Way of an Anthropologist. New York: W. W. Norton, 1966.

19. Slater, Miriam K. African Odyssey: An Anthropological Adventure. Garden City: NY: Doubleday, 1976. Interesting narrative of the author's fieldwork among the Nyika tribe in Tanzania.

20. Thomas, Elizabeth Marshall. The Harmless People. New York: Random House, 1958. Passionate description of a Bushman band. An intimate look at life in the Kalahari Desert.

21. Turnbull, Colin M. The Forest People. New York: Simon and Schuster, 1968. A fascinating, almost novelistic account of Turnbull's field experience among the Pygmies of the Ituri Forest in central Africa (Zaire) that students will almost certainly enjoy. Fits well with the Haviland text.

22. Turnbull, Colin M. The Mountain People. New York: Simon and Schuster, 1972. Absorbing, chilling, controversial account of the Ik of Uganda. The Ik were forced to move to an area when they were unable to adapt, and the book shows how they coped (or did not cope) with a totally new environment.

23. Wilson, Carter. Crazy February: Death and Life in the Mayan Highlands of Mexico. Berkeley: University of California Press, 1974 (originally published in 1965). Basically a novel about a traditional peasant-Indian community, its structure, and the changes that are taking place. Excellent portrayals of typical indigenous characters in peasant communities.

24. Wilson, Peter J. Oscar: An Inquiry into the Nature of Sanity. Would fit well with Chapter 5 in the Haviland text, on culture and personality. It portrays the story of a man named Oscar Bryan who lives on a Caribbean island and whom people believe is insane. The book provides much insight into the nature of insanity and the role nonconformists have in human societies.

Monographs in Paperback Editions to Accompany the Text

1. Applebaum, Herbert. Royal Blue: The Culture of Construction Workers. New York: Holt, Rinehart and Winston, 1981. The main emphasis of this book is on the technological and social organization of the construction industry. The phenomena studied are analyzed from both the cultural and structural-functional viewpoints.

2. Barth, Fredrik. Nomads of South Persia: The Basseri Tribe of the Kamseh Confederacy. Boston: Little, Brown, 1961. Would supplement material on the pastoral adaptation.

3. Benedict, Ruth. Patterns of Culture. New York: New American Library, 1955 (originally published in 1935). Benedict's configurational approach is evident in her much-criticized but still interesting analysis of three

cultures: Zuni, Kwakiutl, and Dobu, all of which are mentioned in the Haviland text.

4. Berdan, Frances F. The Aztecs of Central Mexico: An Imperial Society. New York: Holt, Rinehart and Winston, 1981. Very interesting study of Aztec culture and society; most of which is devoted to an ethnographic reconstruction of the period preceding the conquest.

5. Bodley, John H. Anthropology and Contemporary Human Problems. Palo Alto, CA: Mayfield Publishing Co., 1985. Although not an ethnography, would fit very well with all the themes of Haviland's Chapter 15 on the future. It is especially critical of the "culture of consumption" of industrial societies.

6. Bodley, John. Victims of Progress. Palo Alto: Mayfield Press, 1984.

7. Chagnon, Napoleon. Yanomamo: The Fierce People. Third Edition. New York: Holt, Rinehart and Winston, 1983. Excellent ethnography, well-written in all aspects. Deals with Amazonian Indian tribe on the Orinoco River in Venezuela. Brings us up-to-date on what is happening to them. There are many fine ethnographic films to accompany the book, and the Haviland text refers to this culture often.

8. Daner, Jean Francine. The American Children of Krsna: A Study of the Hare Krsna Movement. New York: Holt, Rinehart and Winston, 1976. This is a fascinating monograph covering all the traditional aspects of ethnographies. The Hare Krsna movement is a total institution for American youths who have become disenchanted with the present social system. It would fit well with discussions on revitalization movements.

9. Dozier, Edward P. The Pueblo Indians of North America. Prospect Heights, IL: Waveland Press, 1970. Good discussion of the modern pueblos. Fits especially well with Haviland's Chapter 14, Culture Change.

10. Evans-Pritchard, E. E. Witchcraft, Oracles, and Magic among the Azande, Abridged Edition. Oxford: Clarendon Press, 1976. This classic work, published in 1937, has just been reissued in paperback form and would be an excellent choice to illustrate religious beliefs among this central African people.

11. Evans-Pritchard, E. E. The Nuer: A Description of the Modes of Livelihood and Political Institutions of a Nilotic People. Oxford: Oxford University Press, 1940. The pastoral Nuer have one of the classic examples of the segmentary lineage system. Well-written ethnography of

this southern Sudan tribe. The very good film, The Nuer, could accompany this book.

12. Foster, George M. Tzinzuntzan: Mexican Peasants in a Changing World. Boston: Little, Brown, 1967. Classic study of a Mexican peasant community. The Image of the Limited Good hypothesis is explained and applied. Has an added section on culture change. Would go well with the films Tepotzlan and Tepotzlan in Transition.

13. Friedl, Ernestine. Vasilika: A Village in Modern Greece. New York: Holt, Rinehart and Winston, 1962. Good book for describing the socio-economic and cultural organization of peasant communities. It would also fit well with Haviland's Chapter 7, Economic Systems.

14. Gamst, Frederick C. The Hoghead: An Industrial Ethnology of the Locomotive Engineer. New York: Holt, Rinehart and Winston, 1980. Approached from an anthropological viewpoint, this study provides the reader with a feeling of realism and directness that is rare in the literature of anthropology.

15. Harris, Marvin. Cows, Pigs, Wars and Witches: The Riddles of Culture. New York: Random House, 1974. The author takes a strict cultural ecological approach to analyze several major "riddles of culture." These include the potlatch, the Tsembaga Maring rumbim rituals, the Inquisition, witchcraft, Christianity, cargo cults, and so forth. Could be used in several ways to illustrate various points brought out by Haviland.

16. Hart, C. W. M. and Arnold R. Pilling. The Tiwi of North Australia. New York: Holt, Rinehart and Winston, 1960. Very interesting study of this northern Australian hunting-gathering culture. Fieldwork Edition, 1979, also available.

17. Heider, Karl G. Grand Valley Dani: Peaceful Warriors. Holt, Rinehart and Winston, 1979. The author introduces us to the Dani by telling about his fieldwork, his ethical dilemmas, and the circumstances of his contact with the Dani.

18. Hoebel, E. Adamson. The Cheyennes: Indians of the Great Plains. New York: Holt, Rinehart and Winston, 1960. Would be very useful to illustrate the chapter on social control, as well as to provide ethnographic data on the Plains Indians.

19. Hostetler, John and Gertrude Huntington. Children in Amish Society. New York: Holt, Rinehart and Winston, 1971. The Amish represent one group of people that have refused to become fully integrated into American society and have

succeeded in remaining relatively independent.

20. Jacobson, David. <u>Itinerant</u> <u>Townsmen</u>: <u>Friendship</u> <u>and</u> <u>Social</u> <u>Order</u> <u>in</u> <u>Urban</u> <u>Uganda</u>. Menlo Park, CA: Cummings, 1973. A readable, urban anthropology ethnography that documents the differing adaptations being made in Uganda to urbanization.

21. Keesing, Robert. '<u>Elota's</u> <u>Story</u>: <u>The</u> <u>Life</u> <u>and</u> <u>Times</u> <u>of</u> <u>a</u> <u>Solomon</u> <u>Islands</u> <u>Big</u> <u>Man</u>. New York: Holt, Rinehart and Winston, 1983. This case study is about the Kwaio, a Melanesian people of the Solomon Islands, as understood through the life history of one remarkable but not atypical Kwaio person named 'Elota.

22. Kluckhohn, Clyde. <u>Navaho</u> <u>Witchcraft</u>. Boston: Beacon Press, 1944. Another classic monograph on witchcraft that would fit well with Chapter 12, Religion and Magic.

23. Lowie, Robert H. <u>The</u> <u>Crow</u> <u>Indians</u>. New York: Holt, Rinehart and Winston, 1956. Classic ethnography of the aboriginal Crow Indian culture. Good example of a matrilineal society.

24. Magnarella, Paul. <u>Traditions</u> <u>and</u> <u>Change</u> <u>in</u> <u>a</u> <u>Turkish</u> <u>Town</u>. Somerset, NJ: Halsted Press, 1974. Good book for culture change topic.

25. Malinowski, Bronislaw. <u>Argonauts</u> <u>of</u> <u>the</u> <u>Western</u> <u>Pacific</u>. New York: E. P. Dutton, 1961. The still-great 1922 classic of one of the founding fathers of modern academic anthropology. Malinowski is mentioned so often in all introductory courses that one of his ethnographies would be a good choice. This one also discusses the famed "Kula Ring" exchange system of the Trobriand Islanders.

26. McFee, Malcolm. <u>Modern</u> <u>Blackfeet</u>: <u>Montanans</u> <u>on</u> <u>a</u> <u>Reservation</u>. Prospect Heights, IL: Waveland Press, 1972. This excellent monograph deals with political organization.

27. Mead, Margaret. <u>Sex</u> <u>and</u> <u>Temperament</u> <u>in</u> <u>Three</u> <u>Primitive</u> <u>Societies</u>. New York: Morrow, 1963 (originally published in 1935). Still interesting study of three New Guinea cultures. Would fit well with the Haviland chapters on culture and personality and economic organization.

28. Metraux, Alfred. <u>The</u> <u>History</u> <u>of</u> <u>the</u> <u>Incas</u>. New York: Schocken Books, 1969. Well-written description of the Inca empire in the Andes.

29. Murphy, Yolanda and Robert F. Murphy. <u>Women</u> <u>of</u> <u>the</u> <u>Forest</u>. New York: Columbia University Press, 1974. The Murphys describe the daily life of the Amazonian Mundurucu. They take several Mundurucu myths and analyze them for their

significance in terms of the tribal social structure. The final chapters compare the role of women in Mundurucu society with the role of women in American society.

30. Nash, Manning. Machine Age Maya: The Industrialization of a Guatemalan Community. Chicago: University of Chicago Press, 1967. Describes the successful adaptation of rural peasant and farmers to the establishment of a large textile mill nearby. Would provide stimulating discussion on the topic of culture change.

31. Newman, Philip L. Knowing the Gurumba. New York: Holt, Rinehart and Winston, 1965. Excellent study, well-written, contrasts with approach taken by Pospisil and Rappaport.

32. Ortiz, Alfonso. The Tewa World. Chicago: University of Chicago Press, 1969. Very well-written study of the Tewa belief system, one of the few truly dual-organization societies. Takes a Levi-Straussian approach.

33. Partridge, William L. The Hippie Ghetto. New York: Holt, Rinehart and Winston, 1973. Would fit with the chapters on marriage and family functions, and culture change. Describes hippie groups in a university town in Florida.

34. Pospisil, Leopold. The Kapuku Papuans of West New Guinea. New York: Holt, Rinehart and Winston, 1978. Another classic often mentioned by Haviland. Author's formal economic perspective contrasts with perspective of a number of other ethnographies of people in the same area, e.g., Rappaport, cited below.

35. Rappaport, Roy A. Pigs for the Ancestors: Ritual in the Ecology of a New Guinea People. New Haven: Yale University Press, 1968. The Tsembaga Maring are the subject of this study. Although perhaps a bit technical for some introductory students using Haviland, it is well-written and is one of the best ecological studies in cultural anthropology.

36. Reichel-Dolmatoff, Gerardo. Amazonian Cosmos: The Sexual and Religious Symbolism of the Tukano Indians. Chicago: University of Chicago Press, 1971. Takes a Levi-Straussian approach to the study of human societies. This group is in the Colombian Amazon region. This work is somewhat more difficult than others, but is well worth it.

37. Rohner, Ronald P. and Evelyn C. Rohner. The Kwakiutl: Indians of British Columbia. New York: Holt, Rinehart and Winston, 1970. Although the Kawkiutl no longer live as they did in the 1800s, the Rohners have done a good job in giving us a very useful and readable description of their former life-style. Since they had a chiefdom, a hunting-gathering-fishing economy and the famous potlatch,

this book would illustrate well a number of concepts in the Haviland text.

38. Spradley, James P. You Owe Yourself a Drunk: An Ethnography of Urban Nomads. Boston: Little, Brown and Company, 1970. Important study of law, values and non-conformists in the United States.

39. Turnbull, Colin M. The Mbuti Pygmies: Change and Adaptation. New York: Holt, Rinehart and Winston, 1983. This excellent case study describes the Mbuti way of life and the sanctuary furnished them by the Ituri Forest, their existence under colonialism and their relations with the villagers, the destructive years of war, and the situation now, since independence.

40. Uchendu, Victor. The Ibo of Southeast Nigeria. New York: Holt, Rinehart and Winston, 1965. Written by an anthropologist who is himself an Ibo, this ethnography describes a patrilineal society with many interesting features.

41. Vogt, Evon Z. The Zincantecos of Mexico: A Modern Maya Way of Life. New York: Holt, Rinehart and Winston, 1970. Excellent monograph, though somewhat abbreviated, on a Mayan community in the State of Chiapas, the subject of the Harvard Chiapas Project.

42. Wong, Bernard. Chinatown: Economic Adaptation and Ethnic Identity of the Chinese. New York: Holt, Rinehart and Winston, 1982. This case study analyzes the structural adaptation Chinese American communities in general, and the New York Chinatown in particular, have made to survive in American society.

FILMS

Although an annotated list of films to use with each chapter of the Haviland text accompanies the related chapter in the Instructor's Manual, a listing of reference works, media resource centers, and film distributors is presented here with the hope that it will be of help in organizing, locating, and ordering instructional media supplements for your course. Films are particularly useful in introductory cultural anthropology courses to provide a visual context for the many cultures and concepts that are being considered. Besides being particularly helpful when it comes to illustrating a culture or concept, they can also be used to stimulate discussion or to develop analytical skills among the students. In each case, however, the students need to be prepared before the screening. Although a large percentage of the films appear to be unbiased and primarily descriptive, in reality they are always the result of much editing, and the filmmakers' biases are often quite evident. This alone can be the subject of stimulating discussions in the classroom. It is suggested that the instructor should at least preview the films before showing them to the class in order to be able to tell the students what to look for. There are written supplements available for some films that are listed in the following indexes, and they are noted. It is frequently advisable to have the students read the supplements both before and after the screening whenever they are available.

Susan Parman of Santa Ana College has developed a technique of "film essays" to help her students beome more critical in their viewing of anthropology films. While the students view a film, Professor Parman projects on a wall questions about it. At the conclusion of the film the students write a one or two paragraph short "essay" answering the questions. Parman believes "this is not a testing method but an educational method."

Faces of Culture

A superb media accompaniment to the Haviland text is the Faces of Culture learning system, consisting of twenty-six one-half-hour television programs and a coordinated study-guide which integrates the print and video components. Of the twenty-six video programs, eighteen are multicultural in their approach, while eight deal exclusively with ethnographic studies of such societies as the Aymara Indians of the Bolivian Andes and the Asmats of New Guinea. Dr. Haviland is technical consultant to the series. The video programs are:

1. The Nature of Anthropology
2. The Nature of Culture
3. How Cultures Are Studied: The Ethnographer
4. How Cultures Are Studied: Archaeology
5. Patterns of Subsistence: Hunters-Gatherers and Pastoralists
6. Patterns of Subsistence: Horticulture and Agriculture
7. Language and Communication
8. Psychological Anthropology I
9. Psychological Anthropology II
10. Marriage and the Family
11. Marriage and Family: A Case Study of the Ycatec Maya
12. Kinship and Descent I
13. Kinship and Descent II

14. Age, Common Interest and Stratification
15. Social Stratification: A Case Study of the Bolivian Aymara
16. Economics
17. Economics: A Case Study of the Highland Maya
18. Political Organization
19. Social Control
20. Religion and Magic
21. Religion and Magic: A Case Study of the Asmat
22. The Arts
23. Mardi Gras: A Case Study of the Arts
24. Culture Change
25. Culture Change: A Case Study of the Trobriands
26. Modernization and Anthropology

For details of leasing or previewing the Faces of Culture series, write: Coast Telecourses, 10231 Slater Avenue, Fountain Valley, CA 92708.

General References

1. American Anthropologist. This journal of the American Anthropological Association systematically carries media reviews. All or almost all of the films mentioned in the film index which follows probably have been reviewed or will be reviewed in this journal. The address is 1703 New Hampshire Avenue, N.W., Washington, D.C. 20009.

2. Heider, Karl G. Films for Anthropological Teaching. Seventh Edition, 1983. This catalog lists and describes 1,575 films used by anthropologists in teaching. Includes film titles, descriptions, bibliographies, prices, and distributors. (For American Anthropological Association members, $10.00; for all others, $15.00) Address is: 1703 New Hampshire Avenue, N.W., Washington, D.C., 20009.

3. Horr, David Agee, ed. "Primate Films." American Anthropologist, 75, December 1973: 1985-2035. Contains about eighty film reviews on the topic and would be extremely valuable for the chapters which deal with primates and the evolution of culture.

1. Audio-Text Cassettes, Center for Cassette Studies, 8110 Webb Ave., North Hollywood, CA 91605. There are over 5,000 cassettes to choose from, although only a few hundred may be directly pertinent for classroom use in an introductory anthropology course. Write for a Reference Catalogue.

2. Education Development Center, 39 Chapel Street, Newton, MA, 02158. This organization produced the excellent film series on the Netsilik Eskimos of Pelly Bay, Canada. The films were directed by Professor Asen Balikci of the Universite de Montreal. There are nine films in the series which deals with the daily activities of this group of Eskimos over an entire year. Some of the films have a natural soundtrack with no narration. All or some of them could be used in any number of introductory courses in anthropology.

3. Encyclopedia Cinematographica of the Audio-Visual Services, 6 Willard Building, Pennsylvania State University, University Park, PA 16802. An international collection of scientific films of cultures all over the world.

4. Documentary Educational Resources, 24 Dane Street, Somerville, MA 02143. This organization owns complete copies of the !Kung Bushman and the Yanomamo film series, with supplementary study guides.

5. Films on Africa, African Studies Program, Indiana University, Bloomington, IN 47401. A descriptive list compiled in 1977 of films held by the Indiana University Audio-visual Center and the African Studies Research Collection is available from the program.

6. Pacifica Tape Library, Pacifica Foundation, Department N A 76, 6316 Venice Blvd., Los Angeles, CA 90019. Contains many cassette tapes that may be useful in the classroom. Brochures describing individual programs are available.

7. Wheelock Educational Resources, P.O. Box 451, Hanover, NH 03755. This organization distributes purchase and rental copies of the American Universities Field Staff (AUFS) Faces of Change with supplementary study guides for each of the twenty-six films available. The series deals with the issue of socio-cultural change in five rural areas of the world: Bolivian Aymara peasants; the agricultural town of Aq Kupruk, Afghanistan; the pastoral Boran of Kenya; the villages and fishermen of the Soko Islands off the coast of China, near Hong Kong; and the rice-producing town of Ts'ao-tun, Taiwan.

Film Distributors

ACC/PH   Appleton-Century-Crofts (now owned by Prentice-Hall Media), 150 White Plains Road, Tarrytown, New York, 10591.

B&C   B & C Films, 3971 Murietta Avenue, Sherman Oaks, CA 91423.

CRM/MH   CRM/McGraw-Hill, 110 15th Street, Del Mar, CA 92014.

DA   Documents Associates, Inc., 211 East 43rd St., New York, NY 10017.

DER   Documentary Education Resources, 24 Dane St., Somerville, MA 02143.

ENMU   Eastern New Mexico University, Portales, NM 88130.

EAV   Educational Audio Visual, Pleasantville, NY 10570.

EDC   Education Development Center, 39 Chapel St., Newton, MA 02160.

FIM/RF   Film Images (a division of Radim Films, Inc.) 4530 18th St., San Francisco, CA 94114.

GP   Grove Press, Film Division, 53 East 11th St., New York, NY 10003.

HFF   Hartley Film Foundation, Cat Rock Road, Cos Cob, CT 06807.

HPI   Heritage Productions, Inc., Harleysville, PA 19438.

IFM   International Film Bureau, Inc., 332 South Michigan Avenue, Chicago, IL 60604.

IUAVC   Indiana University Audio-Visual Center, Bloomington, IN 47401.

NYU   New York University Film Library, 26 Washington Place, New York, NY 10003.

PC   Pacific Cinematheque, 1616 W. 3rd Avenue, Vancouver, B.C., Canada.

PF   Phoenix Films, Inc., 470 Park Avenue, South, New York, NY 10016.

PSU/PCR   PCR Films, Pennsylvania State University, Audio Visual Services, 17 Willard Building, University Park, PA 16802.

T-L	Time-Life Films, Time and Life Building, Rockefeller Center, New York, NY 10020.
TFC	Tricontinental Film Center, 333 Avenue of the Americas, New York, NY 10014.
UCEMC	University of California Extension Media Center, 2223 Fulton St., Berkeley, CA 94720.
UEVA	Universal Education and Visual Arts, Inc., 221 Park Avenue South, New York, NY 10003.
USC	University of South Carolina, Instructional Services Center, Columbia, SC 29208.
WER	Wheelock Educational Resources, P.O. Box 451, Hanover, NH 03755.

Chapter 1

THE NATURE OF ANTHROPOLOGY

Whereas the sociologist or the political scientist might examine the beauty of a flower petal by petal, the anthropologist is the person that stands on the top of the mountain and looks at the beauty of the field.

Robert Gordon

SUPPLEMENTARY NOTES AND OBJECTIVES

Unfortunately, many students arrive in their introductory cultural anthropology class devoid of any conception of what anthropology is about. Some are there because the single open slot in their class schedule happened to be at the time the cultural anthropology class was being offered. Others are there because the introductory sociology section is closed, or perhaps they needed a class dealing with non-Western peoples to satisfy a general education requirement.

The anthropology instructor's best friend at this time is the discipline of anthropology itself. Compared to the academic drudgery of some college courses, anthropology is inherently exciting. William Haviland's opening chapter should give quick notice to those students who stumbled into the class for want of another offering that they have fallen on good fortune.

This initial chapter will dispel the popular notion held by some students in the class that the typical anthropologist wears a pith helmet or an Indiana Jones hat and spends an entire career unearthing stones and bones with a trusty trowel and camel hair brush. Many students will for the first time discover that not all anthropologists are "diggers," and that in addition to archeologists, there are physical anthropologists, linguists, ethnologists, and ethnographers. They will also learn that contrary to the popular image of the ethnographic field-worker working among far-off exotic peoples and with ancient traditional cultures, many of today's anthropologists are doing research "in their own back yard" and with contemporary life.

In addition, Haviland will introduce the student to cross-cultural research, a vital mainstay of cultural anthropology, and an approach that clearly separates it from other disciplines.

1

This chapter provides the instructor with an excellent opportunity to discuss the recent controversy over Mead's research in Samoa. A brief, but excellent discussion of Derek Freeman's controversial critique of Mead's classic work may be found in Science, Vol. 219, March 1983, pp. 1042-1045.

Although anthropology employs the scientific method in its systematic study of the human species and its works, past and present, students should react warmly to Haviland's statement about anthropologists at the end of this chapter:

> Above all, they intend to avoid allowing a "coldly" scientific approach to blind them to the fact that the human species is made up of individuals with rich assortments of emotions and aspirations which demand respect. Anthropology has sometimes been called the most human of the sciences, a designation in which anthropologists take considerable pride.

After Completing Chapter 1, the Student Should Be Able To:

1. Define anthropology and describe the three basic divisions within cultural anthropology.

2. Describe the ethnologist's approach to fieldwork.

3. Describe anthropology's commitment to both the scientific method and humanism.

4. Discuss the importance of cross-cultural research.

CLASS ACTIVITIES/APPLICATION

1. In order to confirm Haviland's point that anthropologists look for the broad basis of human behavior, assign your students the task of asking three professors (an anthropologist, plus two individuals selected from psychology, sociology, economics, geography, or biology) to comment on how they would approach such problems as pollution, overpopulation, food shortage, or birth control. The students should notice that the anthropologist will reflect his or her concern with non-Western societies.

2. Have the class conduct a "garbage study" of their own. A community study would be too complex and involved for a one-semester cultural class, but a simpler version could be conducted on the campus itself. Garbage cans are everywhere: student union building, cafeterias, hallways, bathrooms, classrooms, offices, grounds, etc. Garbage cans

in different areas of the campus should be compared: does the contents of the Psychology Building cans differ from the P.E. cans? English Department cans from the Home Ec cans? The assignment could range from a simple two-to-three day "dig" to a full-semester project.

SUGGESTED FILMS

1. Spirit of Ethnography. PSU/PCR, 18 min., color, 1974. Humorous satire on ethnographic fieldwork and various classic ethnographic films.

2. Yanomamo: A Multidisciplinary Study. USC, 43 min., color, 1971. An excellent film that would be useful for opening the course. It presents the findings of a multidisciplinary research team that investigated the Yanomamo Indians, who are located on tributaries of the Orinoco River in Venezuela. It gives examples of how field research is carried out in the areas of ethnology, linguistics, and physical anthropology.

3. 4-Butte-1: A Lesson in Archeology. USC, 33 min., color, 1968. Field techniques of excavation are illustrated in this archeological study of a Maidu village site in California.

4. Liebela. UCEMC, 58 min., b/w, 1935. In 1935 anthropologist Margaret Hubbard made this film of the Lozi of what is now Zambia. The reissued 16 mm print with added soundtrack is useful in illustrating the difficulty of evaluating another culture without interjecting one's own values.

5. A Man Called Bee: Studying the Yanomamo. USC, 40 min., color, 1975. An excellent film that depicts Napoleon Chagnon engaged in his fieldwork among the same Yanomamo presented in film No. 2 above.

6. Margaret Mead. T-L, 27 min., b/w. Wide-ranging interview with one of the most famous anthropologists. A good film to get a discussion going on the development of anthropology as an academic discipline.

7. Bushmen of the Kalahari (Parts 1 and 2). PSU/PCR, 50 min., color, 1975. This powerful film documents filmmaker-anthropologist John Marshall's return visit to the !Kung Bushmen he studied fifteen years earlier. Excellent film to accompany an introductory discussion of anthropologists in the field.

Chapter 2

THE NATURE OF CULTURE

SUPPLEMENTARY NOTES AND OBJECTIVES

In terms of the entire course, this chapter on the Nature of Culture is probably one of the most important in the book. Accordingly, it is of great value at the outset that the student understand Haviland's definition of culture:

> Culture is a set of rules or standards shared by members of a society that when acted upon by the members, produce behavior that falls within a range the members consider proper and acceptable.

Haviland has mercifully chosen not to dissect any of the 100 plus definitions of culture cited in Kroeber and Kluckhohn's 1952 work; instead, he has expanded on the four basic characteristics that all cultures share. By learning that culture is shared, learned, based on symbols, and integrated, beginning students in anthropology will understand and appreciate the nature and function of culture around the world.

When Haviland discusses the importance of anthropologists studying other cultures in order to determine the difference between cultural ideals and the way people really do behave, students should grasp not only the cross-cultural principle, but also be reminded of its relevance to their own lives in contemporary American society. Indeed, the great appeal of anthropology is the universality of its precepts. Do not miss a chance to remind students of this as you progress through the course and the text.

A question frequently asked by students is, which culture is best? Anthropology has traditionally responded by referring to two concepts, ethnocentrism and cultural relativism. The chapter ends with a discussion of these extreme viewpoints and the need to examine each culture in terms of its success in surviving.

After Completing Chapter 2, the Student Should Be Able To:

1. Define culture and describe how it is studied in the field.
2. Define and describe the four basic characteristics of culture: learned, shared, based on symbols, and integrated.

3. Explain the linkage between culture and process and explain how adaptation and change are important aspects of human culture.

4. Compare and contrast ethnocentrism with cultural relativism.

CLASS ACTIVITIES/APPLICATIONS

1. Have the students conduct a mini-ethnographic field study on the campus or within the community (fraternities, sororities, athletic events, bowling alleys, mobile home parks, dormitories, funeral homes, church services, police and fire departments -- the possibilities are endless). The focus should be on the student observing a situation as a person from another culture might. Ask the students to keep field notes. You may want them to also use a camera and/or tape recorder. A cautionary word: unleashing untrained "ethnographers" can sometimes be hazardous. A few hours devoted to a discussion of field work would be well worth the time and effort.

2. Have students form into small groups (3-5). Through group discussion have students describe three examples of cultural ideals drawn from our culture and three examples of behavior that contrast with the cultural ideals. This exercise will generate much discussion and will reveal the relevancy of anthropological concepts to their own lives.

FILM SUGGESTIONS

1. Salamanders: A Night at the Phi Delta House. UCEMC, 15 min., color, 1982. A superb film to remind students that certain customs in our culture are just as repugnant and/or strange as those they perceive to be so in so-called "primitive" cultures. (In this case, a fraternity ritual of swallowing live salamanders.)

2. Ishi in Two Worlds. PSU/PCR, 19 min., color, 1967. Describes the story of Ishi, the last Yahi Indian, when he emerged from his forest refuge in northern California in 1911. Useful also in mentioning the work of A. L. Kroeber, a major anthropological figure, who allowed Ishi to stay at the Museum of Anthropology of the University of California until his death in 1916.

3. The Children Know. WER, 33 min., color, 1975. Part of the Faces of Change series. This is another excellent and accurate film about the role of formal education in rural areas of the developing world. This one focuses on the Bolivian Aymara community of Vitocota.

4. The Amish: A People of Preservation. HPI, 52 min., color, 1975. Describes the history, world view, simplicity of lifestyle, learning, family, farming, play, and nature of the Amish in Lancaster County, Pennsylvania.

5. Yesterday, Today: The Netsilik Eskimo. EDC, 57 min., color, 1975. Excellent film that brings us up to date on Netsilik Eskimo culture.

6. Margaret Mead. ENMU, 30 min., b/w, 1952. An outstanding anthropologist discusses contemporary world problems. A somewhat dated film, but Mead's observations on education, marriage, the responsibilities of nationhood, and the role of the individual in a democratic society are important to chapter two.

Chapter 3

THE BEGINNINGS OF HUMAN CULTURE

SUPPLEMENTARY NOTES AND OBJECTIVES

> It was just as well, though the face should not be
> mocked. In three hundred million years it would be
> our own.
>
> Loren Eiseley

In this chapter, Haviland notes that one can question the
value of studying non-human primates when it is humans that
are the central topic of cultural anthropology. But he reminds
the reader that humans did not start out as cultural beings,
or for that matter, even as humans. With this in mind, the
chapter discusses the early forerunners of humanity,
Ramapithecines, Australopithecus, Homo erectus, Neanderthals,
and Cro-Magnon, emphasizing the selective advantage that
development of cultural capabilities had for human survival
and adaptation to varied environments.

Through the popular press and various television specials,
most students are at least aware of the several studies of
chimpanzees and gorillas, but few know about other sub-human
primates and the fossil hominids discussed in this chapter.
There are several excellent books that you might suggest to
students for help in this area, but highly recommended are any
of the several written by Stephen Jay Gould (The Panda's
Thumb, 1980; The Mismeasure of Man, 1981; Hen's Teeth and
Horses' Toes, 1983; and The Flamingo's Smile, 1985; all
published by Norton Publishing Company). Loren Eiseley's The
Immense Journey should also be at the top of a recommended
list of highly readable books on physical and behavioral
evolution (Modern Library, 1957).

Because the subject matter in Chapter 3 is largely ignored in
the nation's high schools, the instructor will find it
judicious to cover in the lectures much of the same material
discussed in the text. Students are generally enthralled with
the subject, however, and a carefully guided tour through the
early years of human evolution may even win a few recruits for
your colleague's course in physical anthropology.

After Completing Chapter 3, the Student Should Be Able To:

1. Describe the basic anatomical features of all primates.

2. Describe the most important primate ancestors that preceded <u>Homo</u> <u>sapiens</u> <u>sapiens</u> (Ramapithecines, <u>Australopithecus</u>, <u>Homo</u> <u>erectus</u>, and Neanderthal).

3. Describe the cultural capabilities of the two <u>Homo</u> <u>sapiens</u> ancestors (Neanderthal and Cro-Magnon) of modern day humans (<u>Homo</u> <u>sapiens</u> <u>sapiens</u>).

4. Explain what the author means when he states that during the upper Paleolithic, culture became a more potent force than biology.

CLASS ACTIVITIES/APPLICATIONS

1. Grooming is a notable activity of all primates. Have your students keep a one-week log of examples of grooming behavior on the campus. Ask them to determine if each example is a gesture of friendliness, submission, appeasement, or closeness.

2. Students are especially interested in the similarities and differences between humans and the lower primates. A field trip to a nearby zoo or museum is usually a welcome assignment. Students may be also assigned to watch the occasional television documentaries on lower primates, or asked to view primate films from your college film library which were not shown in class.

SUGGESTED FILMS

1. <u>Monkeys, Apes and Man</u>. USC, 53 min., color, 1971. Provides an overview of research in primatology and the relationship to our understanding of the evolution of human behavior.

2. <u>4-Butte-1: A Lesson in Archeology</u>. USC, 33 min., color, 1968. Field techniques of excavation are illustrated in this archeological study of a Maidu village site in California.

3. <u>Blades and Pressure Flaking</u>. USC, 21 min., color, 1969. Depicts the making of stone blades by direct percussion and by the punch method. Also demonstrates pressure-flaking techniques.

4. <u>Miss Goodall and the Wild Chimpanzees</u>. PSU/PCR, 28 min., color, 1966. Shows how chimpanzees are capable of making and using primitive tools. Also depicts ethnological fieldwork and is one of the classic films in the field of primatology.

5. Lascaux: Cradle of Man's Art. PSU/PCR, 17 min., color. Shows the discovery of cave paintings that date back to Paleolithic times.

6. Mountain Gorilla. UCEMC, 16 min., color, 1959. A study of mountain gorilla behavior in Africa. Very good introductory film detailing aspects of gorilla behavior.

7. Early Stone Tools. PSU/PCR, 20 min., color, 1967. The development of tools is shown to parallel hominid evolution. Several Neanderthal sites are shown. Very good film that would fit well with the text material.

8. Tobias on the Evolution of Man. PSU/PCR, 17 min., color, 1975. Phillip Tobias, the noted paleontologist, traces the evolution of humans. Discusses and shows fossil remains of Australopithecines.

Chapter 4

LANGUAGE AND COMMUNICATION

SUPPLEMENTARY NOTES AND OBJECTIVES

Chapter 4 discusses human language in terms of its fundamental characteristics, the methods used in studying it descriptively, historically, and cross-culturally, and its relationship with the cultural setting in which it is spoken. A brief overview of kinesics, paralanguage, ethnolinguistics, and language origin is also given.

Language is a system for the communication, in symbols, of any kind of information. Through language we translate our concern, beliefs, and perceptions into symbols that can be interpreted by others. Weston La Barre, in his book, The Human Animal (Chicago: University of Chicago Press, 1955: 207), captured the biological and cultural wonder of human language:

> One stands astounded at the world-creation inherent in every language and symbolic system. One stands aghast at the improbability of the whole intricate biological process. Viewed from the unimaginative infra-human side of the line, it is a positive miracle that man has wrought. Homo sapiens, that improbable biped, was never more improbable an animal than in his invention of symbolism. And from the safely human side of the line, one wonders admiringly. How could all these precarious and necessary biological contingencies have been so carefully and artfully assembled?

There are presently in the world 3,000 different languages in existence. Haviland reminds us of the importance of realizing that these languages are spoken by people in societies, each of which has its own distinctive culture. Ethnolinguistics is the field concerned with every aspect of the structure and use of language that has anything to do with society, culture, and human behavior.

In connection with ethnolinguistics, this chapter introduces students to one of the truly seminal concepts in anthropology, the Whorfian Hypothesis, whereby language is seen as a shaping force which predisposes people to see the world in a certain way. The opposite viewpoint is that language reflects reality. One is reminded here of another observation by Weston La Barre in The Human Animal (Chicago: University of Chicago Press, 1955: 207):

10

Indeed, without language, it is safe to say man would never become fully human. But now that he has language, will he ever be able to know reality?

After Completing Chapter 4, the Student Should Be Able To:

1. Describe thte nature of human language, distinguishing it from the communication system of other animals.

2. Discuss the steps a descriptive linguist takes in analyzing a language (phonology, morphology, syntax, grammar, and lexicon).

3. Discuss the relationship between language and culture and language and thought.

4. Discuss what is known about the origin of speech.

CLASS ACTIVITIES/APPLICATION

1. Ask your students to interview and then contrast the different patterns of speech (vocabulary, gestures, code switching, etc.) exhibited by elderly people and, say, "New Wave" or "punk" youth in the local area. The activity could be continued by asking individuals in each group to decipher the utterances of the other.

2. Divide the class into all-male and all-female teams, with each team compiling a list of taboo words, obscenities, and unacceptable language they feel is specific to their sex. For a comparison of the lists, have the teams write their words on the chalkboard.

SUGGESTED FILMS

1. Verbal Communication: The Power of Words. UCEMC, 20 min., color, 1982. Excellent film to help students understand the important relationship between culture and language.

2. In Search of a Mate. ENMU, 24 min., color, 1972. Insects to mammals are observed in this film in ordr to learn how signals, postures, colors, and sounds are used in mating.

3. Invisible Walls. USC, 12 min., b/w, 1969. Investigates the physical distance that Americans perceive should be maintained around themselves. Good film, emphasizing nonverbal communication.

4. <u>Without Words: An Introduction to Nonverbal Communication</u>. PH, 23 min., color, 1977. Shows several aspects of nonverbal communication (proxemics, kinesics, etc.) including an examination of cross-cultural nonverbal barriers. Excellent film.

5. <u>The Ancient Egyptian</u>. PSU/PCR, 27 min., color, 1963. The history of Egypt is traced from prehistoric times to the present with an excellent portion devoted to the development of hieroglyphic writing. Could also be used to illustrate persuasiveness of early diffusionist theories that had Egypt as the ultimate source of all human inventions.

6. <u>Teaching Sign Language to the Chimpanzee Washoe</u>. PSU/PCR, 48 min., b/w, 1973. Important film graphically depicting the rationale and describing some of the successes of the Gardners' experiment with Washoe.

.Chapter 5

CULTURE AND PERSONALITY

SUPPLEMENTARY NOTES AND OBJECTIVES

> . . . psychologizing is a deeply rooted habit among
> cultural anthropologists.
>
> Marvin Harris

Psychological anthropology, or culture and personality, is an area of research where the field of cultural anthropology relates to the psychology of personality. In other words, it is the coming together of anthropology and psychology. Carrying a heavy load of Freudian principles, the field got off to a rocky start in America during the late 1920s and 1930s. The movement emphasized the human element in culture and sought from the beginning to validate its findings by cross-cultural comparisons. Psychological anthropology addresses two main types of questions: What are people like from one society to another? How did they get that way?

This chapter provides many examples of the inextricable relationship between one's culture and one's personality. Haviland discusses the major areas within the field: the self and the behavioral environment, enculturation, individual and group personality, modal personality, national character, and abnormal personality. Introduced is the thinking of several key figures in pyschological anthropology: Margaret Mead, Anthony F. C. Wallace, Sigmund Freud, John Whiting, Irvin Child, Ruth Benedict, Geoffrey Gorer, and A. Irving Hallowell.

Students generally have an immense interest in the subject matter of psychological anthropology. Most have taken the basic psychology course on campus, and a few have taken abnormal psychology. Both courses give little or no attention to normal and abnormal personalities in non-Western cultures. This is definitely an opportunity for anthropologists to lend a helping hand to our brethren in the psychology department.

Noting that the early work in culture and personality was subjected to heavy fire for being impressionistic rather than scientific, Haviland reminds us that anthropologists have established that cultures are indeed different and that their members possess personalities reflecting these differences. He concludes with a brief discussion of the current culture and personality studies that combine traditional psychoanalytically-based theories with biological and social factors to explain culture and cultural dynamics.

Because the history of psychological anthropology is riddled with contradictory data and misunderstanding, it would be wise for the instructor who may be shy on background in Culture and Personality to dig a little before approaching the material in class. An excellent source for such an excursion is Marvin Harris' The Rise of Anthropological Theory (New York: Thomas Y. Crowell Co., 1968: Chapters 15-17), wherein the ups and downs of Culture and Personality are nicely chronicled. Another good general source is Victor Barnouw, Culture and Personality (Homewood: Dorsey Press, 1985, 4th ed.). In the latter source, Barnouw (1979: 4) laments on the difficulty of defining the terms culture and personality because of their popular usage with older colloquial meanings which run counter to those given in the social sciences ("He has a lot of culture, but she's the one with the compelling personality"). Philip K. Bock's Continuities in Psychological Anthropology (San Francisco: W. H. Freeman and Co., 1980) will also be useful.

After Completing Chapter 5, the Student Should Be Able To:

1. Describe the relationship between the self and the behavioral environment.

2. Define the concept of personality as used by anthropologists.

3. Discuss the major objections to national character studies.

4. Show that the concept of "normality" can be meaningful only within the context of a given culture.

CLASS ACTIVITIES/APPLICATIONS

1. Here's a good exercise to illustrate widespread beliefs in national stereotypes -- most of which are transmitted by media. Divide the class into small groups, assigning each a country of origin (China, Russia, U.S.A., Iran, France, Germany). Each group will construct a "national character" and ask the other groups to attempt to identify their nationality. This will be an ideal time for the instructor to expand on Haviland's discussion of the concept of national character.

2. Ask your students to observe a mother-child interaction and a father-child interaction. Have them analyze these interactions to determine how they differ (verbal, touch, gestures, closeness, etc.) and write a paper on their findings.

SUGGESTED FILMS

1. <u>Rivers</u> <u>of</u> <u>Sand</u>. PF, 84 min., color, 1974. Examines traditional sex roles among the Hamar of southwestern Ethiopia.

2. <u>Kalogeros</u>. UCEMC, 12 min., b/w, 1969. A documentary of a fertility ritual in the village of Kalogeros in northern Greece. It gives background to the Benedict idea of a Dionysian cultural configuration.

3. <u>Personality</u> <u>in</u> <u>Culture</u>. IUAVC, 29 min., b/w. Gives some background to Japanese personality and culture that might be helpful in explaining the Japanese national character studies discussed in the text.

4. <u>Arrow</u> <u>Game</u>. PSU/PCR, 7 min., color, 1974. Depicts Yanomamo boys being encouraged to become "fierce." Boys are seen engaging in a mock arrow fight where they learn how to dodge arrows and shoot accurately. Fits the themes of enculturation and basic personality in the text.

5. <u>Sociobiolgy</u>. DA, 20 min., color, n.d. A survey of this new and controversial field that discusses the behavioral responses of humans to biology and natural selection.

6. <u>Margaret</u> <u>Mead's</u> <u>New</u> <u>Guinea</u> <u>Journal</u>. IUAVC, 90 min., color, 1968. Mead narrates the film about her return trip to Peri Village, Manus Island, in Polynesia in 1967. Covers many aspects pertinent to a discussion of life cycle, but it is also important because of the significant changes that have taken place since her original trip in 1928.

7. <u>Children</u> <u>of</u> <u>Bet</u> <u>Alpha</u>. PF, 27 min., color, 1974. Gives a peaceful and interesting view of child-rearing practices in an Israeli kibbutz. Focuses on infants, three-year-olds, seven-year-olds, and twelve-year-olds. Persuasive film that will encourage much discussion. Could also be used and/or linked with later text chapters on family organization.

8. <u>Garcons</u> <u>et</u> <u>Filles</u>. N.C./FISCT, 30 min., b/w, 1965. Portrays the initiation ceremonies of young Ghaya boys and girls.

Chapter 6

PATTERNS OF SUBSISTENCE

SUPPLEMENTARY NOTES AND OBJECTIVES

Human adaptation takes place within a biological and social environment. The complex relationship humans have with them produces varying cultural responses. This chapter focuses on these relationships and examines in detail four major adaptaive responses: hunting-gathering, horticulture, pastoralism, and intensive agriculture.

Chapter 6 provides the instructor with a golden opportunity to show the relevance of anthropology to contemporary life, namely through Haviland's timely discussion of adaptation. Haviland points out that in adaptation there is a moving balance between a society's needs and its environmental potential. Adaptation also refers to the interaction of an organism and its environments, with each causing change in the other. With the ongoing struggle between pro- and anti-forces of such current conflicts as nuclear power plants, off-shore oil drilling, save-the-whales (dolphins, baby harp seals, etc.), industrial pollution, fluoridation of water, and the like, students will find this chapter to be not only of great interest; but also validation of Chapter one's commentary on the usefulness of anthropology in modern-day life.

Haviland's explanation of the general concept of adaptation is given depth through a discussion of Julian Steward's terms: culture type (the view of a culture in terms of its particular technology to the environment exploited by that technology), culture core (the features of a culture that play a part in matters relating to the society's way of making a living within it), and the work of certain anthropologists known as ethnoscientists.

The author quotes anthropologist Marshall Sahlins as describing hunter-gatherers as the "original affluent society." Haviland explains the quote, but for further enlightenment on the now discredited idea that a hunting-gathering life was difficult and that one had to work hard just to stay alive, see Marvin Harris, Cannibals and Kings: The Origins of Cultures (New York: Random House, 1977). Harris argues convincingly that hunters of the upper Paleolithic period (30,000 B.C. to 10,000 B.C.) enjoyed relatively high standards of comfort and security. He also maintains that hunters and gatherers built superior shelters, were unusually well-nourished, did not have to work around the clock to feed themselves, and had little interest in giving up the nomadic life to live in villages. Haviland's conclusion is instructive: ". . . hunters and gatherers in the world today are not following an ancient way of life because they don't know any better, they are doing it through deliberate choice."

Haviland's discussion of the role of women in hunting and gathering societies provides us with another excellent opportunity to remind students of the relevance of anthropology to modern-day life.

A few words of explanation may be helpful in regard to Haviland's use of the term !Kung in this chapter and elsewhere in the text. Many anthropologists have adopted the term "San" for the people because they feel !Kung Bushmen is demeaning. The word "Bushman" is in fact not derogatory. It derives from the Dutch word "bossiesman," which means "bandit." The Bushmen were called bandits because of their refusal to submit to colonial authority. The irony is, <u>San</u> means <u>Bushman</u>. Haviland prefers to use a people's own name for themselves, hence, !Kung appears in the text.

After Completing Chapter 6, the Student Should Be Able To:

1. Explain adaptation as it refers to how humans interact with the environment in order to provide the basic needs of food and shelter.

2. Describe what is meant by evolutionary adaptation.

3. Contrast food-producing societies with hunting-gathering societies.

4. Compare and contrast the subsistence patterns of hunters and gatherers, horticulturalists, and pastoralists.

5. Show the relationship between intensive agriculture and the rise of cities.

CLASS ACTIVITIES/APPLICATIONS

1. Cultural adaptation has enabled humans to survive and expand in a variety of environments. As an exercise in helping your students understand how they have adapted to the sociopolitical environment of the college, have them keep a detailed one-week log of their travel on the campus and in the community, and the ways in which they dealt with the contingencies of daily life.

2. Ask your students to write a short paper on how their life would change if they had to live without such basic items of technology as television, telephones, refrigerators, hot and cold running water, and automobiles.

SUGGESTED FILMS

1. The Gods Must Be Crazy. Twentieth Century Fox, 109 min., color, 1980. A funny to some, but upsetting to others, commercial movie. The Bushmen scenes were filmed at Tshumkwe, the subject of the text for Portfolio One. The people of Tshumkwe are also cited in Chapter 16 as a people who are dying out as a result of repressive government policies. The hero of the film is Xi, a Bushman from the Kalahari Desert of Botswana. The character Xi is portrayed by Kalahari Bushman N!Xau. Watch for it at local theatres or videotape stores.

2. The Kiliwa: Hunters and Gatherers of Baja, California. UCEMC, 15 min., color, 1975. Excellent film to expand on Haviland's discussion of the balance between a society's needs and its environmental potential.

3. The Hunters. IUAVC, 72 min., color, 1968. One of the classic ethnographies on film. Depicts a band of Kalahari Bushmen in daily activities and shows four of them hunting a giraffe. Demonstrates how resourceful humans can be even in very difficult environments. The Bushmen are frequently mentioned in the Haviland text.

4. The Desert People. CRM/MH, 51 min., b/w, 1968. This prize-winning film gives a vivid picture of a group of aborigines hunting and foraging in the Central Australian desert.

5. Nanook of the North. IUAVC, 55 min., b/w, 1922. Robert Flaherty's simply wonderful film about an Eskimo family hunting and gathering in the Hudson Bay region. A must for every undergraduate student.

6. Winter Sea Ice Camp: Parts I, II, III, IV. (Part of the Netsilik Eskimo Series; see distributor for additional titles.) UEVA, 30 min. each, color. Excellent series of films depicting the Netsilik Eskimos. In these segments the Eskimos are seen trekking across sea ice, building igloos, playing games, in trials of strength for men, cooking, and so forth. No narration.

7. The Nuer. IUAVC, 70 min., color, 1970. Another beautiful film. This concerns the pastoral Nuer of the Southern Sudan in their daily round of activities. There is not enough narration to make the film totally comprehensible to students. If Evans-Pritchard's The Nuer is used, it would work well.

8. Dani Sweet Potatoes. UCEMC, 19 min., color, 1974. Very good film about the horticultural practices of the Dugum Dani of the New Guinea Highlands. It was shot among the same people who appear in the long film Dead Birds, mentioned in the film index under Chapter 11.

9. Slash and Burn Agriculture. ENMU, 20 min., color, 1976. A forest is slashed down, cultivated with crops, and then burned. Ten years later it may be used again after it has grown back.

Chapter 7

ECONOMIC SYSTEMS

SUPPLEMENTARY NOTES AND OBJECTIVES

In this chapter, Haviland describes economic systems as the outgrowth of human subsistence strategies, which themselves are the result of the interactions between humans and their environment. Every economic system must have regulations regarding production, consumption, and distribution. Although culture remains an important variable, every society has a division of labor and rules determining access to land and technology.

In times past, the chapter on economic systems in an introductory cultural anthropology text was often considered by students to be one of the least interesting chapters in the book. However, today's students are vitally interested in the subjects discussed in Chapter 7, and for good reason. The difficulties of surviving in an economy with double-digit inflation along with an aversion to huge, impersonal, industrial corporations and their products, places in a new and favorable light such subjects as craft specialization, reciprocity, barter and trade, conspicuous consumption, and other economic strategies discussed by Haviland.

In references to the sexual division of labor in human societies, Haviland believes only a few broad generalizations can be made covering the kinds of work performed by men and women. Anthropology is in an ideal position to shed light on the subject of the sexual division of labor because of its cross-cultural approach. Ironically, it is this very approach that can also clutter any understanding of the subject. Given one's stance on the matter of the "proper" role of each sex in the division of labor, one may simply invoke an example from the ethnographic record to affirm or negate a given argument. Ernestine Friedl believes arguments about the proper role of sex:

> . . . will never be settled as long as the opposing sides toss examples from the world's cultures at each other like intellectual stones. (Human Nature, April 1978.)

You may wish to assign for reading the above article by Friedl, as it is an excellent piece to spark a discussion on sex roles in economic systems. Other useful sources here are Carol MacCormack and Marilyn Strathern, Nature, Culture, and Gender (Cambridge University Press, 1980), and Martin King Whytes, The Status of Women in Preindustrial Societies (Princeton University Press, 1978).

After Completing Chapter 7, the Student Should Be Able To:

1. Describe the area of study known as economic anthropology.

2. Cite the basic resources a society needs to be able to produce desired goods and services.

3. Explain how the sexual division of labor enters into the allotment of work.

4. Describe reciprocity systems of exchange, redistribution systems of exchange, and market exchange.

CLASS ACTIVITIES/APPLICATIONS

1. Ask the students to write a brief paper on which kinds of goods are exchanged among their friends (e.g., labor skills, material objects, nonmaterial property). Is there evidence of reciprocity, redistribution, bartering?

2. Have your students observe and then write a brief paper (or give an oral report) on the exchange patterns present in birthday parties, marriage, holiday gifts, and in bars.

SUGGESTED FILMS

1. The Turtle People. B&C, 26 min., color, 1973. Excellent film about the changing economic system of the Miskito Indians of the Nicaraguan Caribbean coast. Shows the ecological consequences of selling subsistence resources (turtles). Study guide is available from B&C.

2. To Live with Herds. FIM/RF, 68 min., b/w, 1973. Provides a very good, realistic background to the life of pastoralists. The culture presented here is of the Jie people of northeastern Uganda.

3. Island in the China Sea. WER, 32 min., color, 1975. Tai A Chau, one of the Soko Islands near Hong Kong, is home for both farmers and fishermen. The daily routines of both are depicted. Part of the Faces of Change film series. Study guide is available from WER.

4. China Coast Fishing. WER, 19 min., color, 1975. Focuses on the fascinating adaptation the Soko Island "boatpeople"

have made to heir environment. Part of the Faces of Change film series. Study guide is available from WER.

5. An Afghan Village. WER, 44 min., color, 1975. Part of the Faces of Change film series. Presents a collage of daily life in the town of Aq Kapruk in northern Afghanistan. Good sequences of the sports and entertainment of the villagers. Study guide is available from WER.

6. Afghan Nomads: The "Maldar." WER, 21 min., color, 1975. Should be shown in conjunction with An Afghan Village (above). Shows a caravan of sheep herders interacting with the Aq Kapruk villagers between whom there is mistrust. Part of the Faces of Change film series. Study guide is available from WER.

7. A Strict Law Bids Us Dance. PC, 1975. Kwakiutl view of their potlatch and the history of the suppression of it by the Canadian government.

8. The Water Is So Clear That a Blind Man Could See. IV. 30 min., color, 1970. Documents the struggle between New Mexico's Taos Indians and various lumber companies over the Blue Lake area.

Chapter 8

MARRIAGE AND THE FAMILY

SUPPLEMENTARY NOTES AND OBJECTIVES

Families are immensely important in most societies of the world, and the social order is regulated through systems in which families are linked by ties of marriage between their members. In Chapter 8, we learn about the close interconnection between marriage and the family, with Haviland telling us there are as many different family patterns as the fertile human imagination can invent.

Although we do not usually think of a family as being engaged in economic cooperation, the author provides us with considerable data to support his belief that the primary importance of the family is to provide for economic cooperation between the sexes while also providing a proper setting where child-rearing may occur.

In spite of the so-called "new morality" in the United States and Canada, there is still a strong belief here, as elsewhere in the world, that marriage should occur before a family is started. (Historically speaking, the reverse order of events holds true: it is the family that came first, with marriage growing out of it. After all, the family is a biological universal among humans, while marriage is strictly a matter of culture.) This chapter shows us that the form of family and marriage organization is determined by the specific kinds of problems people must solve in particular environments.

The major marriage and family areas in Haviland's Chapter 8 are: functions of the family, control of sexual relations, form of the family, marriage, and problems of family organization. Within these major areas, Haviland offers us a cross-cultural view of nurturance of children, rules of sexual access, the incest taboo, endogamy and exogamy, the levirate and sororate, monogamy, polygyny, polyandry, serial marriage, divorce, the extended family, residence patterns, bride price, and bride service.

This chapter provides a vital bridge to Chapter 9, Kinship and Descent.

After Completing Chapter 8, the Student Should Be Able To:

1. Explain the nurturance functions of the family in human societies.

2. Explain how and why the family functions to control sexual relations in human society.

3. Describe what is universal about the human family and cite its basic forms.

4. Define marriage and cite its basic variants.

5. Show how the extended family differs from the nuclear family.

CLASS ACTIVITIES/APPLICATIONS

1. Ask your class to imagine that polygamy, polyandry, bride price, the levirate and the sororate are to become instituionalized in American culture. Divide the class according to sex and ask each group to argue the advantages and disadvantages of the "new system" for each sex.

2. Ask any students who were raised in a serial marriage family if they would be willing to discuss in class the advantages and disadvantages of this increasingly common pattern of marriage.

SUGGESTED FILMS

1. Boran Women. WER, 18 min., color, 1974. Part of the Faces of Change film series. The pastoral Boran women appear to have more power than the Afghan women. Study guide is available from WER.

2. An Argument about a Marriage. USC, 18 min., color, 1966. A dispute arises in a !Kung Bushman band over the legitimacy of a marriage. Study guide is available from DER.

3. Afghan Women. WER, 17 min., color, 1975. Part of the Faces of Change film series. Shows rural women engaged in daily activities and conversation. Interesting also for insight into the purdah custom (isolating women from the public arena). Study guide is available from WER.

4. Andean Women. WER, 17 min., color, 1975. Part of the Faces of Change film series. The Aymara women depicted here are very interesting for their activities and beliefs regarding their role in society. Study guide is available from WER.

5. Bride Service. PSU/PCR, 10 min., color, 1975. This film gives an example of the bride service institution among the Yanomamo Indians. Study sheet available from DER.

6. A Father Washes His Children. PSU/PCR, 15 min., color, 1974. Dedeheiva, a Yanomamo shaman, takes his nine children to the river and washes them carefully. Study sheet is available from DER.

7. Rivers of Sand. PF, 84 min., color, 1974. Examines marriage and sex roles among the Hamar of southwestern Ethiopia.

8. Kypseli: Women and Men Apart--A Divided Reality. UCEMC, 40 min., color, 1977. Depicts how the peasants of Kypseli, a small Greek village, divide space, time, and activities. The social structure is related to the prevalent view of women as dangerous and threatening.

Chapter 9

KINSHIP AND DESCENT

SUPPLEMENTARY NOTES AND OBJECTIVES

In the last chapter we learned that family organization is the principal means for dealing with basic human problems. In Chapter 9, Haviland tells us that many societies need to deal with problems that are beyond the scope of the family, for example, defense, allocation of resources, and provision of cooperative work forces for tasks too large for a family. In nonindustrial societies these tasks are frequently met through kinship groups. Haviland introduces this chapter with a brief but excellent description of the functions of kinship groups:

> In societies where a great number of people are linked by kinship, these groups serve the important function of precisely defining the social roles of their members. In this way, they reduce the potential for tension that might arise from the sudden and unexpected behavior of an individual. They also provide their members with material security and psychological support through religious and ceremonial activities.

Throughout the history of anthropology, the study of kinship has been a principal subject of anthropological inquiry. The reason is simple: the bonds of kinship are the most fundamental of all social bonds.

In the last chapter students learned about the various modes of marriage. In this chapter they will learn a basic fact of social organization shared by people the world over: when a person marries the "one and only," he or she has also "married" a stack of relatives as well. Marriage is much too important for the survival of the group to be left to the marrying couple alone.

The heart of Chapter 9 is the descent group: a publicly recognized social entity which has as its criterion of membership, descent from a common ancestor through a series of parent-child links. Haviland introduces students to unilineal, double, and ambilineal descent. He also describes the various forms of descent groups: Lineages, clans, phratries, and moieties. The principle of bilateral kinship, a characteristic of Western society, is also explained. The chapter ends with a description of kinship terminology and kinship groups.

In perfect adherence to the anthropological commitment to cross-cultural studies, Haviland's Chapter 9 provides the student with a perspective on kinship organization gleaned from ten different non-Western cultures.

After Completing Chapter 9, the Student Should Be Able To:

1. Define descent groups and show how they function in societies without formal political systems.

2. Compare matrilineal with patrilineal descent systems.

3. Describe the main elements of lineages, clans, phratries, and moieties.

4. Describe bilateral kinship.

5. Describe the basic kinship terminologies found in the world: Iroquois, Omaha, Crow, Hawaiian, Eskimo, and Descriptive.

CLASS ACTIVITIES/APPLICATIONS

1. In this exercise, class members are asked to collect genealogies on each other, which then serve as a basis for kinship analysis and diagramming. After you have lectured on kinship and the students have read Chapter 9, assign each class member a partner. (Ask students to change partners if they are familiar with each other's family background.) Each partner is to interview the other in an attempt to construct a kinship chart for that person. A basic rule is for the respondent to provide only information asked for and not to volunteer data.

2. A variation of the above exercise is to have students construct a kinship chart of their own family, using themselves as ego. This exercise can be made more interesting by expanding its scope into a semester-long project where the students construct a thorough family genealogy. This would necessitate interviewing nearby relatives as well as corresponding with out-of-staters and asking for old and new photographs of family members as well as photos of family tombstones in their area. (Photographs make the assignment more interesting, especially when placed in a family album along with the genealogy.) A good motivation technique is to remind the students that the genealogies they are assembling more than likely will be the only one in existence--now and in the future for the family.

SUGGESTED FILMS

1. <u>Mbambim</u>: <u>A</u> <u>Lineage</u> <u>Head</u> <u>in</u> <u>Ayikpere</u>, <u>North</u> <u>Togo</u>. SWF, 23 min., b/w, 1973. Focuses on the headman of a patrilineage who is having difficulty commanding authority within his lineage.

2. <u>A</u> <u>Joking</u> <u>Relationship</u>. USC, 13 min., b/w, 1966. Shows the play and banter of a !Kung Bushman man and woman.

3. <u>Ax</u> <u>Fight</u>. PSU/PCR, 30 min., color, 1975. This film shows how conflicts can easily erupt in large Yanomamo villages. A slow-motion replay provides commentary. There is a part that explains the fight in terms of the kinship structure. Study sheet is available from DER.

4. <u>Tapir</u> <u>Distribution</u>. PSU/PCR, 15 min., color, 1975. Shows the distribution of meat along the kinship structure to restore the shaken alliance interrupted by an ax fight. Study sheet is available from DER.

5. <u>A</u> <u>Man</u> <u>Called</u> <u>Bee</u>: <u>Studying</u> <u>the</u> <u>Yanomamo</u>. DER, 40 min., color, 1971: Shows anthropologist Napoleon Chagnon engaged in fieldwork with the Yanomamo of Venezuela. Kinship structure of the Yanomamo is described.

Chapter 10

AGE, COMMON INTEREST, AND STRATIFICATION

SUPPLEMENTARY NOTES AND OBJECTIVES

As important as kinship ties are in regulating and controlling the life of many of the world's peoples, they cannot provide for all the organizational needs of a society. As traditional ways of life give way to new ones, kinship becomes less effective in meeting such needs and is replaced by other forms of social organization.

In this chapter, Haviland tells us about age groupings, common interest associations, and stratification systems based on class and caste. The cross-cultural examples supplied by the author show the immense variety of these three forms of nonkinship social organizations and make fascinating reading, partly because reading about other cultures is inherently interesting, but also because students can reflect on their own experiences in this culture with such groupings. Haviland states:

> . . . age grouping is so familiar and so important that it and sex have sometimes been called the only universal factors in the determination of one's position in society.

Today's students will bring to this chapter a far different set of experiences with its subject matter than, say, a student of ten years ago. During the last decade this country has witnessed deep and far-reaching changes in social practice and thought related to age, sex, and social class distinctions. Elementary school sports programs are coeducational by government fiat; exclusive men's clubs are becoming anachronisms; all-male universities have admitted women, and vice-versa. Arbitrary age barriers for retirement, legal drinking, voting, and the like are challenged daily. The examples are endless. The point is: the students in your anthropology classes are, as never before, able to appreciate the subject matter of this chapter.

Haviland raises the yet unresolved questions as to why women are barred from associations in some societies, while in others they participate on an equal basis with men. Before addressing yourself to the problem in class, it would be judicious to read one or all of these books: Ernestine Friedl, _Women_ _and_ _Men:_ _An_ _Anthropologist's_ _View_ (Holt,

29

Rinehart and Winston, 1970), Rayna Reiter, ed., Toward an Anthropology of Women (Monthly Review Press, 1975), Alice Schlegel, ed., Sexual Stratification: A Cross-Cultural View (Columbia University Press, 1977). Martin King Whyte, The Status of Women in Preindustrial Societies (Princeton University Press, 1978), and Carol MacCormack and Marilyn Strathern, Nature, Culture, and Gender (Cambridge University Press, 1980).

After Completing Chapter 10, the Student Should Be Able To:

1. Describe the role of age-groupings in society.

2. Describe common-interest associations and how they arise in human societies.

3. Discuss social stratification.

4. Contrast class and caste and describe their functions in stratified societies.

5. Discuss the concept of mobility.

CLASS ACTIVITIES/APPLICATIONS

1. Divide the students into teams. Tell them that they are going on an expedition to the Kalahari Desert, and they will have to make a list of important items to take with them. The interesting part of this exercise is how their "survival" list will vary depending on age, sex, occupational backgrounds, and social class.

2. Have the students analyze their friendship with three of their closest friends. How is the friendship dependent on age, sex, common interest associations, and stratification.

SUGGESTED FILMS

1. Garcons et Filles. ENMU, 30 min., b/w, 1968. Portrays the initiation ceremonies of young Ghaya boys and girls of the Bouar-Baboua region (near the Yade Range).

2. Deep Hearts. FSC, Harvard, 50 min., color, 1979. This fine film focuses on the Gerewol ritual, a ceremonial pageant where West African young men, wearing women's clothing, strive to be selected as the most beautiful.

3. The Rural Cooperative. WER, 15 min., color, 1975. Part of the Faces of Change film series. Describes a farmer's association in Taiwan. Study guide is available from WER.

4. North Indian Village. UCEMC, 30 min., color, 1958. Though somewhat old, it is a good film to illustrate the Indian caste system.

5. Ku Klux Klan: The Invisible Empire. UCEMC, 47 min., b/w, 1965. A television documentary that describes the history, development and present nature of this common-interest association.

6. Sky Chief. UCEMC, 26 min., color, 1972. Depicts the meeting and interaction of three social groups--Indians, mestizos, and oil workers--in the Equadorean Amazon. Also useful for Chapter 14, on culture change.

7. India: Writings on the Sand. UCEMC, 30 min., color, 1964. Discusses the social problems which interrelate with the population problem. Presents illuminating accounts of major aspects of life in contemporary India, including the caste system.

Chapter 11

POLITICAL ORGANIZATION AND SOCIAL CONTROL

SUPPLEMENTARY NOTES AND OBJECTIVES

Every society must have means by which conflicts can be resolved and decisions made which are acceptable to the people who must live by them. Political systems and social control are two major cultural mechanisms by which societies seek to overcome the forces of fragmentation and achieve integration.

In Chapter 11, Haviland describes and analyzes four basic types of political systems that have been identified, ranging in order of complexity from uncentralized bands and tribes to centralized chiefdoms and states.

In reference to social control, the author writes:

> Whatever form the political organization of a society may take, and whatever else it may do, it is always involved in one way or another with social control. Always it seeks to ensure that people behave in acceptable ways, and defines the proper action to take when they don't.

According to Haviland, social controls are either internalized (guilt, shame, fear of divine punishment, magical retaliation) or externalized (sanctions). Law, a key to the efficient functioning of political organizations and social control, serves several basic functions: it defines relationships and thereby aids its own efficient operations by ensuring that there is room for change, and it allocates authority to employ coercion in the enforcement of sanctions.

In essence, this is a chapter about power, for the exercise of authority (power) is a constant phenomenon in human societies. If we concur that society and order are synonymous, then it follows that authority, or power, serves as the foundation of the order which society exhibits.

Haviland ends Chapter 11 with a discussion of two topics inextricably related to the subject at hand (both of which, although high on this culture's list of tabooed dinner table topics, are guaranteed "sparkers" in the classroom): war and religion.

After Completing Chapter 11, the Student Should Be Able To :

1. Describe fully the four basic types of political systems.

2. Describe the functions of law.

3. Discuss the role of warfare in political systems.

4. Define internalized and externalized social controls and discuss their differences.

5. Show how religion is inevitably felt in the political sphere.

CLASS ACTIVITIES/APPLICATIONS

1. Ask your students to describe a quarrel in any group of which they are, or have been a member. They should indicate if the quarrel was settled by peers or higher status members. Was violence involved? Did factionalism or cohesion occur?

2. Have your students visit a courtroom and listen to a judgment rendered in a case, after which they are to show how Pospisil's four basic attributes of law apply: authority, universal applicability, the two-sided nature of every dispute, and the determination of the nature and degree of sanctions. If the courtroom visitation is not feasible, ask the students to apply Pospisil's attributes to the local newspaper's account of three different court cases.

SUGGESTED FILMS

1. Little Injustices. UCEMC, 55 min., color. Excellent film for demonstrating the cross-cultural approach as a means of enlightenment about our own institutions, plus showing the male chauvinists in the classroom about the eminence of women professionals in anthropology.

2. Dead Birds. USC, 84 min., color, 1963. Award-winning film of the Dugum Dani of the New Guinea highlands. It depicts the ritual warfare they are constantly engaged in, their ritual life and mythology. Study guide entitled "The Dani of West Irian" available from Cummings Publishing Co.

3. Magical Death. PSU/PCR, 28 min., color, 1973. Award winning film from the Yanomamo film series. It shows Dedeheiwa, the Yanomamo shaman, in a drug-induced trance attempting to send his Hekura spirit to kill an enemy in order to help stabilize the intergroup alliance. Study sheet is available from DER.

4. <u>Night</u> <u>and</u> <u>Fog</u>. IUAVC, 31 min., color, 1955. This film is a French documentary of the WW II Nazi concentration camps that is at once "beautiful" and brutal. If your students can stand it, they will certainly realize that the terms "primitive" and "savage" are quite ethnocentric.

5. <u>The</u> <u>Cows</u> <u>of</u> <u>Dolo</u> <u>Ken</u> <u>Paye</u>: <u>Resolving</u> <u>Conflicts</u> <u>among</u> <u>the</u> <u>Kpelle</u>. Examines the conflict arising out of the process of modernization taking place in Fokwele, Liberia, through the analysis of an event. The dispute is resolved by the intervention of an ordeal specialist.

6. <u>To</u> <u>Make</u> <u>the</u> <u>Balance</u>. UCEMC, 33 min., color, 1970. Anthropologist Laura Nader's excellent film showing the effectiveness of an unwritten village legal system in Oaxaca, Mexico.

7. <u>You</u> <u>Wasn't</u> <u>Loitering</u>. DER, 15 min., b/w, ca. 1969. Part of the <u>Pittsburgh</u> <u>Police</u> film series. This film is a group of sequences related to the policy and practice of enforcing loitering ordinances in Pittsburgh. Several youths are arrested by the police for loitering.

8. <u>The</u> <u>Ax</u> <u>Fight</u>. DER, 30 min., color, 1971. A four section documentary of an ax fight between two groups of Yanomamo Indians, including an unedited record of the fight, a slow motion replay indentifying the combatants and explaining their behavior, an explanation of the fight as representing the basic cleavages (no pun intended) between local descent groups in the village, and an edited version illustrating how intellectual models influence visual perception.

Chapter 12

RELIGION AND MAGIC

SUPPLEMENTARY NOTES AND OBJECTIVES

The study of cultural beliefs about supernatural beings and powers has been the subject of much anthropological research. Haviland's Chapter 12 is directed toward this research. It is a chapter about religion and magic and the various beliefs and practices which support each: gods and goddesses, ancestral spirits, animism, animatism, priests, shamans, rituals, witchcraft, and ceremonies.

Haviland speaks for all anthropologists when he states:

> Although anthropologists are not qualified to pass judgment on the metaphysical truth of any particular religion, they can attempt to show how each religion embodies a number of "truths" about humans and society.

Looked at in this light, a study of religion will tell us not only about religion itself, but also about humans and their special and psychological needs.

When people are unable to handle problems through technological means, they try to come to grips with them through the control of supernatural beings. In this sense one is reminded of an observation by William Howells in his book, The Heathens: Primitive Man and His Religions (New York: Doubleday and Co., 1956, p. 19):

> . . . the simplest technical exercise, like baiting a hook so that a fish will want to bite it, is scientific, while putting a spell on the same hook and bait to make the fish bite, regardless of his appetite, is religious. Thus people solve their problems either by science or by religion, since, if science hasn't an answer, religion has.

Long ago Malinowski observed that in the Trobriand Islands magic did not occur when the natives fished in the safe lagoons but when they ventured out into the open seas: then the danger and uncertainty caused them to perform extensive magical rituals. For a delightful analysis of the application of magic to this country's "national pastime," see George Gmelch's article, "Baseball Magic" (Human Nature, August 1978, and also Society, vol. 8, no. 8, 1971).

As in most chapters of this book, Haviland provides the student with views of the subject matter from the non-Western world as well as contemporary United States. Thus, students will read about religion and magic among the Dayaks, Tewa, !Kung and Ibibio, Azande, and Navajo, as well as reading about such familiar topics as Muslim and Christian fundamentalism, the Reverend Jim Jones, "Moonies," horoscopes, and ouija boards.

After Completing Chapter 12, the Student Should Be Able To:

1. Define religion and explain the anthropological approach to the study of religion.

2. Distinguish between animism and animatism.

3. Explain the differences between priests/priestesses and shamans.

4. Discuss the two basic categories of rituals.

5. Distinguish between magic, witchcraft, and religion.

CLASS ACTIVITIES/APPLICATIONS

1. Tell your students that they are anthropologists from another culture and that they are to attend a religious service in American culture. Ask them to keep careful notes of the ceremony, layout of the church, furniture, symbols, artifacts, and people in attendance. Armed with this data, they are then to analyze the meaning of what they observed.

2. Students are intrigued with discussing contemporary sects and religious movements, including the Reverend Sun Myung Moon's Unification Church, the cult of the Reverend Jim Jones, Bhagwan Shree Rajneesh, Scientology, UFO cults, and the revival of witchcraft. Ask your class to write a paper on such phenomena.

SUGGESTED FILMS

1. Magical Death. PSU/PCR, 28 min., color, 1973. Award winning film from the Yanomamo series. It shows a shaman in a drug-induced trance attempting to send his spirit to kill an enemy in order to help stabilize intergroup alliance.

2. To Find Our Life: The Peyote Hunt of the Huichols of Mexico. UCLA, 60 min., color, 1970. Documents the peyote hunt of the Huichol Indians. Several religious ceremonies are filmed during the ritual journey into the desert in search of peyote.

3. Holy Ghost People. UCEMC, 53 min., b/w, 1968. Scrabble-Creek, WV, is the setting for this long religious service of a white Pentecostal sect. It is an excellent film depicting snake handling, possession, speaking-in-tongues and general worship. Incidentally, the "preacher" bitten at the end of the film survived the rattlesnake's venom.

4. Sucking Doctor. UCEMC, 30 min., b/w, 1964. Shows, without narration, a healing ceremony of the Kashia group of the Southwestern Pomo Indians. The Indian doctor is Essie Parrish, the last Southwestern Pomo sucking doctor to practice this ancient form of doctoring.

5. N/Um Tchai. USC, 19-1/2 min., b/w, 1966. The curing dance of the !Kung Bushmen. Study sheet is available from DER.

6. Appeals to Santiago. CRM/MH, 28 min., ca. 1967. Exciting film that presents the natives' view of a major peasant religious ceremony. Takes place in a Tzetal Mayan town in the state of Chiapas, Mexico.

7. Magic and Catholicism. WER, 34 min., color, 1975. Part of the Faces of Change series. The film shows the importance of faith and magic among the people of the Bolivian highlands.

Chapter 13

THE ARTS

SUPPLEMENTARY NOTES AND OBJECTIVES

Because art reflects the values and concerns of the people who create and enjoy it, it is properly an area of investigation for anthropology.

We have already read in Haviland about several cultural mechanisms by which societies combat fragmentation and achieve wider integration. In Chapter 13, Haviland views the arts as a kind of behavior that contributes to well-being and helps give shape and significance to life, thereby promoting the overall integration of human societies.

Considering the enormity of the task, the author has wisely chosen not to cover all forms of art--instead concentrates on only a few: verbal arts, music, and sculpture.

Franz Boas, in his classic work, <u>Primitive Art</u> (New York: Dover, 1955, p. 9), helps us appreciate Haviland's belief that art is the creative use of the human imagination to interpret, understand, and enjoy life:

> No people known to us, however hard their lives may be, spend all their time, all their energies in the acquisition of food and shelter, nor do those who live under more favorable conditions and those who are free to devote to other pursuits the time not needed for securing their sustenance occupy themselves with purely industrial work or idle away the days in indolence. Even the poorest tribes have produced work that gives to them esthetic pleasure. . . . In one way or another esthetic pleasure is felt by all members of mankind.

After Completing Chapter 13, the Student Should Be Able To:

1. Define art and explain its function in human society and culture.

2. Cite the basic kinds of verbal arts.

3. Define the meaning and use of myth.

4. Define the meaning and use of legends and tales.

5. Define the elements and functions of music.

CLASS ACTIVITIES/APPLICATIONS

1. Ask each student to interview a foreign student regarding origin myths in their culture. How did they come into being? What beings were instrumental in their culture's creation? How do the creators' powers compare with those of present members of the culture? What features of the present-day culture does the myth explain? How do these features structure life in the culture?

2. The social function of music is perhaps most obvious in song. Ask your students to select five country-western songs and analyze their content. What do they tell us about American attitudes and values toward sex, individualism, loyalty, patriotism, love, authority, God, and self-reliance? It would also be interesting to compare the content of country-western songs with the content of rock or blues songs.

SUGGESTED FILMS

1. Indian Artists of the Southwest. DER, 15 min., color, 1972. Shows Southwestern Indians demonstrating their craft skills. Emphasizes their belief in the unity of man and nature. Includes Zuni stone cutting and setting, Navajo silverwork and weaving, Pueblo pottery, and Hopi Kachina dolls.

2. Dance and Human History. UCEMC, 40 min., color, 1976. A cross-cultural view of dance and its relation to social structure. Excellent film.

3. The Tribal Eye: An Exploration of Tribal Cultures. UCEMC, 7 films in the series, 52 min. each, color, n.d. This is a beautiful set of films that focuses on tribal art in various settings. The cultures represented in them are: Northwest Coast Indians, Dogon of Nigeria (masks), the New Hebrides and the Solomon Islands, Aztec and Inca (gold), Qashqa'i nomads of Iran, and the Benin Kingdom.

4. Bitter Melons. USC, 30 min., color, 1966. This film shows how subsistence activities and social relationships are expressed in traditional music and dances of the !Kung Bushmen. Study sheet is available from DER.

5. Living Stone. UCEMC, 22 min., color. Shows the carving of sculpture by an Eskimo at Cape Dorset, Canada, and its meaning in relation to their religious beliefs.

6. Imaginero. IUAVC, 52 min., color, ca. 1970. The sensitive story of an Indian folk artist living in Northern

39

Argentina. He is both painter and sculptor of essentially religious themes flowing out of his syncretistic Hispanic-Quechua belief system.

7. <u>A History of Popular Music in America</u>. EAV, color filmstrip, 1974. Very enjoyable coverage of popular music from the turn of the century to the 1970s. (Six twenty-minute filmstrips.)

8. <u>Buma</u>: <u>African Sculpture Speaks</u>. UCEMC, 9 min., color, 1952. Native music and pictures of carved masks and statues are used to portray the life of the natives of West Central Africa and to reflect their fundamental fears and emotions.

Chapter 14

CULTURE CHANGE

SUPPLEMENTARY NOTES AND OBJECTIVES

No human group has been able to avoid culture change. Everywhere, most people are confused and threatened by the dynamics of change so swift that one generation stands in astonishment at the one which preceded it. There has always been change, but the rate of change today is staggering, and the challenges of coping with it enormous. Although modern day processes of changes are unique, the basic mechanisms underlying change have remained the same throughout history: invention, diffusion, cultural loss, and acculturation. Each of these mechanisms is examined by the author in Chapter 14, as well as such forced change situations as colonialism, military conquest, rebellion, and revolution. Revitalization movements are also discussed and the chapter ends with a look at modernization, a process of change by which developing societies seek to acquire characteristics of industrially advanced societies. The Shuar Indians of the Amazon forest and the Skolt Lapps serve as contrasting examples of the effects modernization is having on non-Western peoples.

Haviland feels that understanding the dynamics of change is one of the most important and fundamental of anthropological goals. In this connection he writes:

> . . . The more anthropologists study change and learn about the various ways people go about solving their problems of existence, the more aware they become of a great paradox of culture. On the one hand, the basic business of culture is to solve problems, but in doing so, it inevitably creates new problems which themselves demand solution.

By training and interest, the anthropologist is in an ideal position to help diminish the conflicts that inevitably arise when vastly different cultures make contact and the change process occurs. In the last chapter of the book, we will learn that this is an immensely difficult job.

After Completing Chapter 14, the Student Should Be Able To:

1. Explain the principal causes of culture change.

2. Define and explain the term invention as a mechanism of change.

3. Define diffusion and explain how it works.

4. Define acculturation and the variety of forms it may take.

5. Define modernization and what it entails.

CLASS ACTIVITIES/APPLICATIONS

1. As an exercise in understanding revitalization movements, ask your students to create and describe an imaginary culture undergoing a severe culture crisis. The time is ripe for a charismatic leader, a Messiah, to emerge. Ask each student to proclaim himself or herself the leader of the oppressed culture. As the leader, he or she must describe why the existing culture is inadequate, what the new culture will be like, and how converts will be won.

2. Have the class form into several small groups and through discussion each group is to make a list of at least seven social-cultural changes that have occurred in American culture since World War II.

SUGGESTED FILMS

1. The Last Tasmanian. UCEMC, 61 min., color, 1980. Excellent film on genocide.

2. The Children Know. WER, 33 min., color, 1975. Part of the Faces of Change series. This is another excellent and accurate film about the role of formal education in rural areas of the developing world. This one focuses on the Bolivian Aymara community of Vitocota.

3. New Tribes Mission. PSU/PCR, 12 min., color, 1974. An Evangelical Protestant missionary group explains why they must bring Christianity to the Yanomamo. Study sheet is available from WER.

4. Ocamo Is My Town. PSU/PCR, 23 min., color, 1974. This film focuses on the problem of contact that takes place between the West and the Yanomamo Indians. In this case, the West is represented by a Salesian missionary who has lived fourteen years with the Yanomamo.

5. So That Men Are Free. PSU/PCR, 25 min., b/w, 1963. Perhaps the only film made of a successful applied-anthropology project. This one deals with the famed Vicos Cornell-Peru Project begun by anthropologist Alan Holmberg.

6. The Tribe That Hides from Man. IUAVC, 62 min., color, 1973. Very good film that records the work of two Brazilian anthropologists to put Amazonian Indians on

reservations in order to protect them from too-rapid acculturation. Should provoke much discussion among the students.

7. <u>Yesterday, Today: The Netsilik Eskimo</u>. EDC, 57 min., color, 1975. Excellent film that brings us up-to-date on the Netsilik Eskimo.

8. <u>You Are on Indian Land</u>. PSU/PCR, 37 min., ca. 1970. This is a film report of a protest demonstration and eventual confrontation with Canadian authorities by the Mohawk Indians of the St. Regis Reserve over rights that they felt had been denied them.

9. <u>Last Grave at Dimbaga</u>. DER, 55 min., color, 1974. Introduction to South Africa and its racially based social, political, and economic problems.

Chapter 15

THE FUTURE OF HUMANITY

SUPPLEMENTARY NOTES AND OBJECTIVES

> To prophesy is extremely difficult -- especially with
> respect to the future.
>
> (Chinese Proverb)

Although we can appreciate the poignancy of the above proverb,
it would be irresponsible, if not foolish, for anthropologists
to hopelessly turn their backs on their knowledge of the
world's problems and refrain from discussing the importance of
these problems to the future of humanity. Haviland argues in
Chapter 15 that since future forms of culture will be shaped
by decisions humans have yet to make, they cannot be predicted
with any accuracy. Anthropologists, because of their training
and experience, are well-suited to help people understand the
existing world situation. To comprehend anthropology's role in
understanding and solving the problems of the future, Haviland
examines various flaws seen in the vast amount of future-
oriented literature published in the past few decades.

In Chapter 15, Haviland also gives us his viewpoint of what
an anthropologist can tell us about global society and its
problems. He observes that some anthropologists are concerned
that there is a trend for the problems of human existence to
outstrip cultures' ability to find solutions. World-wide, the
survival of the human species is dependent upon conquering the
large problems discussed by Haviland in this chapter: the
concept of the one-world culture, cultural pluralism, the rise
of the multi-nationals, the rejection of modernity,
ethnocentrism, global apartheid, problems of structural
violence, world hunger, pollution, birth control, and the
discontent that springs from the economic gap between poor and
developed countries.

Some anthropologists believe that by the end of this century
the last preliterate tribe will have passed away, also, the
remaining peasant societies will have disappeared. If ever
there were a time in the history of anthropology as a
discipline that anthropologists could sit back and loftily
declare a noninvolvement stance when confronted by a culture's
struggle with the problems discussed by Haviland, that time is
over.

Chapter 15 is based on the premise that however humanity changes biologically, culture remains the chief mechanism by which humans solve their problems of existence. In light of this, we would do well to ponder with our students the last paragraph of Weston La Barre's The Human Animal (Chicago: University of Chicago Press, 1954: 333-334):

> In our new knowledge and power over the atom we wait, it would seem, some new morning for mankind. But at this instant in human history it is already three minutes to midnite. That all our world-views are colored by our human problems and needs, we must all finally admit. But that we struggle with these problems and needs is at least an animal dignity we might all strive to achieve. A billion other worlds may turn, without end and without meaning, in the cold cosmic night. But on this one earth, at least, now live animals able to become even a little like gods, having knowledge of good and evil.

After Completing Chapter 15, the Student Should Be Able To:

1. Discuss the advantages and disadvantages of a "one-world culture."

2. Define and explain cultural pluralism

3. Discuss the relationship between cultural pluralism and ethnocentrism.

4. Discuss the problems of food shortage, population growth, crowding, pollution, and discontent.

CLASS ACTIVITIES/APPLICATIONS

1. Ask your students to select a non-Western culture of their choice and write a research paper on the impact of Westernization on that culture. As a variation, divide the class into small groups, with each group assembling data on Westernization of the culture of its choice and giving a panel presentation of their findings to the class.

2. Using Jules Henry's quote at the beginning of the chapter as a starter, ". . . although culture is 'for' man, it is also 'against' him," ask your students to provide examples from their own life to validate its meaning.

45

SUGGESTED FILMS

Note: Many of the films listed in Ch. 16 would be useful for Ch. 15, too.

1. N!ai: The Story of a !Kung Woman. DER, 58 min., color, 1980. Portrays the life of N!ai from early childhood to middle age, showing how her band is transformed from successful foraging to semi-dependent squatters on a government reservation. N!ai's group is discussed in the text for Portfolio One. The film also shows the filming of the end of "The Gods Must Be Crazy."

2. Future Shock. CRM/MH, 42 min., color, 1972. A good film to use at the end of the course with the Haviland text. This film is based upon Alvin Toffler's best seller of the same title and shows the effect technology is having upon human society.

3. Into the Mouths of Babes. CBS, 29 min., color, 1978. Documents the introduction of an American infant formula into several developing countries by multi-national corporations.

4. The Mountain People. PSU/PCR, 24 min., color, 1974. Sensitive film depicting the plight of rural tenant farmers in the Appalachian region of Tennessee.

5. American Samoa: Paradise Lost? IUAVC, 55 min., color, n.d. Discusses the effects of the Americanization of Samoa on Samoans and their traditional cultural values. Should stimulate much discussion.

6. The Last Tribes of Mindanao. PSU/PCR, 52 min., color. A glimpse of the recently found "Stone Age" Tasaday tribe in the Philippines. Examines what the Tasaday think about their being "discovered."

7. Kenya Boran I & II. WER, 33 min., each, color, 1975. Part of the Faces of Change film series. This good film depicts the pastoral Boran of Kenya in their traditional lifestyles. It also shows their reaction to new Western values that are gradually entering their society through greater government contact and because of larger numbers of children attending school.

8. The Last Tasmanian. UCEMC, 61 min., color, 1980. Excellent film on human genocide.

9. Controlling Interests: The World of Multinational Corporations. California Newsreel, 630 Natoma St., San Francisco, CA 94103, 45 min., color, 1978. Shows the growing impact of multinational corporations and discusses the relationship between growing economic concentration, underdevelopment in the Third World, and U.S. policy towards developing countries.

Chapter 16

THE FUTURE OF ANTHROPOLOGY

SUPPLEMENTARY NOTES AND OBJECTIVES

In this final chapter, Haviland reminds our students that although there are fewer "lost cities" and "missing links" left to discover, it does not mean anthropologists will be left with nothing to do. There is a future for anthropology! Haviland points out that anthropologists will continue to study the traditional way of life in the world's remaining tribal and band societies as well as focus upon the process of modernization as it occurs among these groups. He also notes the increase in anthropological studies of North American culture and expects them to continue into the forseeable future.

Chapter 16 is an impressive accounting of the humanitarian service anthropology has provided in salvaging the endangered societies of the world. Haviland discusses the work of an organization of anthropologists in the United States that is concerned about human rights and the survival of the world's indigenous cultures, Cultural Survival, Inc. Also examined are the disappearing past, genocide, applied archeology, the role of anthropology in emerging modern societies (including North American culture), anthropology and jobs, and questions of ethics in anthropological research and development.

It should be impossible for a student to read this chapter and take seriously this observation from Vine Deloria's Custer Died for Your Sins (New York: Avon Books, 1969, 83-84):

> . . . Into each life, it is said, some rain must fall. Some people have bad horoscopes, others take tips on the stock market. McNamara created TFX and the Edsel. Churches possess the real world. But Indians have been cursed above all other people in history. Indians have anthropologists.

Deloria's comments may be amusing and witty, but such writing is a sad disservice to the academic discipline which has done more for indigenous peoples of the world, American Indians included, than any other academic field. He displays a monumental ignorance of the work and commitment of American anthropologists when he observes in Custer Died for Your Sins (p. 269) that anthropologists should be involved in helping Americans understand equality, that they should serve as volunteers to tribes, use their research skills to help solve real problems, and volunteer before Congressional committees on behalf of Indians. Anthropologists have been doing these things since the 19th century.

It is fitting that the Haviland book concludes with a discussion of ethics. More than ever before, the kinds of research and job opportunities entered into by anthropologists today raise important questions concerning anthropological ethics. In May 1970, the Council of the American Anthropological Association adopted its Statements on Ethics (Principles of Professional Responsibility). The Principles cover six major areas and are regarded as fundamental to the anthropologists' ethical pursuit of their profession. For a full copy of the Statements on Ethics see <u>Anthropology Newsletter</u>, May 1970, v. 19, No. 4.

After Completing Chapter 16, the Student Should Be Able To:

1. Discuss the role of anthropology in the future.

2. Describe how anthropologists are responding to the need for the study of modern societies.

3. Describe the basic ethical concerns of anthropologists.

4. Discuss several nonacademic jobs available for people with anthropological backgrounds.

CLASS ACTIVITIES/APPLICATIONS

1. By the time the students read Chapter 16, the term is probably near the end. An easy but informative assignment would be to have them keep a one- or two-week account from the mass media of any violations that threaten the human rights and survival of indigenous cultures the world over.

2. A similar assignment would be to ask your students to keep a brief account of local environmental discussions revolving about the impact of proposed construction projects on archeological resources in the area.

SUGGESTED FILMS

Note: Many of the films listed in Ch. 15 would be useful for Ch. 16, too.

1. <u>Bushmen of the Kalahari (Parts 1 and 2)</u>. PSU/PCR, 50 min., color, 1975. This powerful film documents anthropologist John Marshall's return visit to the same !Kung Bushmen he filmed fifteen years earlier. Excellent film to accompany a discussion of contributions anthropologists can make to cultures they are studying.

2. So That Men Are Free. CRM/MH, 27 min., b/w, 1965. Describes anthropologist Allan Holmberg's culture change project in Vicos, Peru. The film raises many questions concerning ethics in fieldwork.

3. Hospital. Zipporah Films, 81 min., b/w, 1970. A sobering view of a typical hospital in a contemporary American city. An excellent film to introduce the problems facing the medical anthropologist studying American health care.

4. American Samoa: Paradise Lost? IUAVC, 55 min., color, n.d. Discusses the effects of the Americanization of Samoa on Samoans and their traditional cultural values. Should stimulate much discussion.

5. The Tribe That Hides from Man. IUAVC, 63 min., color, 1973. Shows Brazilian anthropologists attempting to protect Amazonian Indians from rapid acculturation.

6. Margaret Mead: New Guinea Journal. UCEMC, 93 min., color, 1967. Excellent film showing Mead's four decades of work in New Guinea.

7. Last Grave at Dimbaza. DER, 55 min., color, 1974. Introduction to South Africa and its racially based social, political, and economic problems.

CHAPTER 1: THE NATURE OF ANTHROPOLOGY

Multiple Choice Questions

1. Why did it take such a long time for a systematic development of anthropology to appear?
   a. a lack of specific data
   b. no commonly agreed upon theories
   *c. a failure of Europeans to recognize the common ties of humanity
   d. a fear of what the future will hold for man.

2. The first college course in general anthropology was offered at the University of Vermont in:
   a. 1620
   b. 1779
   *c. 1886
   d. 1906.

3. Anthropologists are able to acquire an extensive overview of human beings because they look for:
   *a. the broad basis of human behavior
   b. the intensive narrow basis of human behavior
   c. the religious basis of human behavior
   d. the historical and geographical basis of human behavior.

4. An attempt to view things in the broadest possible context, in order to understand their interconnections and interdependence:
   a. linguistic approach
   b. anthropometry
   *c. holistic perspective
   d. archaeometrics.

5. Physical anthropology is concerned primarily with:
   a. the physical surroundings of a group
   b. how members of a group physically interact
   c. the physical make-up of society
   *d. humans as biological organisms.

6. Which of the following is not a branch of cultural anthropology?
   *a. paleontology
   b. archeology
   c. linguistics
   d. ethnology.

7. By studying the whole of humanity, cultural anthropologists seek to minimize the problem of:
   a. self-fulfilling prophecy
   *b. culture bound theory
   c. limited goods theory
   d. culturology.

8. The social science to which cultural anthropology has
   most often been compared:
   a. history
   b. psychology
   *c. sociology
   d. geography.

9. One of the fundamental principles of anthropology:
   a. etymology
   b. culturology
   c. artistic quantification
   *d. holistic perspective

10. Archeology is the study of:
    a. attitudes about behavior
    b. a society's perception of its values
    c. biological organisms
    *d. material objects.

11. The Arizona Garbage Project was undertaken by:
    *a. archeologists
    b. physical anthropologists
    c. cultural anthropologists
    d. linguists.

12. The branch of cultural anthropology that studies human
    languages:
    a. mass communication
    *b. linguistic anthropology
    c. culturology
    d. oral anthropology.

13. Perhaps the most distinctive human feature is the ability
    to:
    a. walk upright
    *b. speak
    c. stand upright
    d. defend territory.

14. The ethnologist concentrates on:
    a. cultures of the past
    b. cultures of the future
    *c. cultures of the present
    d. unknown cultures.

15. Fundamental to the ethnologist's approach is:
    a. laboratory experimentation
    *b. descriptive ethnography
    c. textual research
    d. artifact examination.

16. Ethnography is also known as:
    a. human variation
    *b. fieldwork
    c. the archeology of human beings
    d. the ethnologic present.

17. The ethnologist becomes an ethnographer by:
    *a. living with the people under study
    b. completing a doctorate in anthropology
    c. publishing the results of the study
    d. applying an archeological analysis.

18. "The_____is an archeologist who catches his archeology alive."
    a. linguist
    *b. ethnographer
    c. physical anthropologist
    d. ethnologist.

19. The archeologist studies the legacy of extinct cultures, some of them as old as:
    a. 1 million years
    *b. 2.5 million years
    c. 4.5 million years
    d. 5 million years.

20. There have always been ethnographers working "in their own backyards." One such person is:
    a. Robert Scott
    b. B. Raymond Druian
    c. Warner L. Williams
    *d. W. Lloyd Warner.

21. May deal with the description of a language or with the history of a language:
    a. phonemics
    b. etymology
    c. diachronics
    *d. linguistics.

22. The chief concern of all anthropologists is the careful and systematic study of:
    a. subhuman primates
    b. non-Western people
    c. present-day people
    *d. humankind.

23. A tentative explanation of the relationship between certain phenomena is known as:
    a. an independent variable
    b. a variable concept
    c. an absolute truth
    *d. a hypothesis.

24. Which of the following is the anthropologist least likely to take into the field?
    a. camera
    *b. questionnaires
    c. tape recorders
    d. first-aid equipment

25. Two basic ingredients of science are imagination and:
    a. dogmatism
    *b. skepticism
    c. perfidy
    d. bombasticism

26. In cross-cultural research, the greater the number of societies being examined, the less likely it is that the investigator will have:
    a. a quick return home
    *b. a detailed understanding of all the societies encompassed by the study
    c. a close relationship with the people in all the societies encompassed by the study
    d. a desire to restudy the people studied.

27. Ideally, theories in cultural anthropology are generated from:
    a. a single culture
    b. regional comparisons
    c. contrasting studies of two different cultures
    *d. world-wide comparisons.

28. A kind of ethnography which studies cultures of the recent past through the accounts of explorers, missionaries, traders, and the analysis of various records:
    a. historical accounting
    *b. ethnohistory
    c. historical determinism
    d. ethnoscience.

29. Ethnologists study:
    a. mainly primitive societies
    b. usually urban societies
    c. seldom their own society
    *d. all human societies.

30. Anthropology has sometimes been called the most:
    a. radical of the sciences
    b. conservative of the sciences
   *c. humanistic of the sciences
    d. systematic of the sciences.

Essay Questions

1. Describe the four branches of the discipline of anthropology.
2. Discuss the relationship between anthropology and the humanities.

CHAPTER 2: THE NATURE OF CULTURE

Multiple Choice Questions

1. Provided the first really clear and comprehensive definition of culture:
   *a. Edward Burnett Tylor
   b. Alfred L. Kroeber
   c. Bronislaw S. Malinowski
   d. David James Ritchie.

2. An acceptable modern definition of culture is:
   a. that complex whole which includes knowledge, belief, art, law, morals, customs, and other capabilities and habits
   b. a group of people dependent on each other for survival
   c. a society which functions as an inter-related whole
   *d. a set of rules or standards that, when acted upon by the members of a society, produce behavior that falls within a range of variance the members consider proper and acceptable.

3. In the 1950s these two anthropologists combed the literature and collected over one hundred definitions of culture:
   a. Mead and Benedict
   b. Boas and Tylor
   *c. Kroeber and Kluckhohn
   d. Powdermaker and Hortense.

4. "A group of people occupying a specific locality who are dependent on each other for survival and who share a common culture" is a:
   a. subculture
   b. culture
   *c. society
   d. populace.

5. Generally, in order for members of a society to understand the behavior of other members, there must be _____ about the meaning of behavior.
   a. rules
   b. discussions among people
   c. announcements
   *d. shared assumptions.

6. The relationships that hold a society together are known as:
   a. social bonding
   b. social networks
   c. social adhesion
   *d. social structure.

7. Which of the following is <u>not</u> a characteristic of culture?
   a. culture is shared
   b. culture is based on symbols
   c. culture is integrated
   *d. culture is innate

8. A society in which subcultural variation is particularly marked is a:
   a. homeostatic society
   b. variable society
   *c. pluralistic society
   d. multi-society.

9. One reason the Amish people may be tolerated more in the United States than the American Indian peoples is the _____ difference between these two societies.
   a. intellectual
   b. spiritual
   c. financial
   *d. racial.

10. The Old Order Amish in the United States are an example of a:
    a. pluralistic society
    b. variable society
    c. world culture
    *d. subculture.

11. The process whereby culture is transmitted from one generation to the next is termed:
    a. indoctrination
    *b. enculturation
    c. heredity
    d. transmission.

12. All culture is:
    a. biologically inherited
    *b. learned
    c. self-destructive
    d. non-integrative.

13. Another way to describe human language is:
    a. the objectifying of beliefs
    b. the use of puns to describe social situations
    c. the substitution of objects for words
   *d. the substitution of words for objects.

14. Leslie White considered all human behavior to originate:
    a. in the chemical substances of cells
   *b. in the use of symbols
    c. in the transmission of nerve signals to the brain
    d. in the society's set of rules.

15. The most important symbolic aspect of culture is:
   *a. language
    b. government
    c. religion
    d. recreation.

16. Among the Kapauku Papuans of New Guinea, political power
    and legal authority is achieved through:
    a. plant cultivation
    b. fishing
   *c. pig breeding
    d. hard work.

17. The process in which all aspects of a culture function as
    an interrelated whole is:
    a. cultural relativism
    b. linguistic nationalism
   *c. integration
    d. historical particularism.

18. Culture:
    a. can be observed directly in the field
   *b. cannot itself be directly observed in the field
    c. is not studied by the ethnologist
    d. cannot be investigated in the field.

19. The possession of characteristics that permit organisms
    to overcome the hazards and secure the resources that
    they need in the particular environments in which they
    live:
    a. variation
   *b. adaptation
    c. environmental possession
    d. genetic adjustment.

20. Napoleon Chagnon studied which of the following people:
    a. Siriono
    b. Dani
    c. !Kung
   *d. Yanomamo.

21. In order to survive, a culture must:
    *a. satisfy the basic needs of its members and provide for
            its biological continuity
    b. strike a balance between the self-interest of
            individuals and the needs of the group
    c. control the environment
    d. cultivate plants.

22. The cultural capacity of apes:
    a. is less impressive than once thought
    *b. is more impressive than once thought
    c. is unable to be scientifically studied
    d. is similar to that of dolphins

23. A deliberate attempt to construct a more satisfying
    culture is known as a:
    a. war
    b. confrontation movement
    c. revolution
    *d. revitalization movement.

24. A tendency to regard one's own culture as better than all
    others is known as:
    *a. ethnocentrism
    b. cultural relativism
    c. kulturpride
    d. ethnicenterness.

25. The ultimate test of a culture is its:
    *a. capability to adapt to new circumstances
    b. ability to feed its people
    c. knowledge of history
    d. tolerance to other peoples.

26. According to the author, science is not entirely value-
    free because:
    *a. science itself is a product of culture
    b. westerners have generally been ethnocentric
    c. westerners have usually tried to view culture from a
            relative point
    d. values are often expensive.

27. The idea that culture can only be judged according to its
    own standards is:
    a. ethnocentrism
    *b. cultural relativism
    c. diffusionism
    d. structuralism.

28. A group functioning within the general confines of the larger culture while observing a set of rules that is somewhat different from the standard:
    a. populace
    *b. subculture
    c. clique
    d. gang.

29. Cultural breakdown may occur if a society does not strike a balance between the self-interest of individuals and:
    a. the economy
    b. the needs of other societies
    *c. the needs of the group
    d. the self-interest of leaders.

30. Used by anthropologists to counter ethnocentric thinking:
    a. self-fulfilling prophecy
    b. phylogenetic theory
    *c. cultural relativism
    d. societal determinism.

Essay Questions

1. Describe the four basic characteristics shared by all cultures.

2. How would an anthropologist respond to a non-anthropologist who has asked the question, "Which culture is best?"

CHAPTER 3: THE BEGINNINGS OF HUMAN CULTURE

Multiple Choice Questions

1. Compared to those of other mammals, primates' teeth are:
   a. more numerous
   b. more specialized
   c. less efficient
   *d. less specialized.

2. Which of the following is incorrect? The primate adaptation to life in the trees coincides with:
   a. a decline in the sense of smell
   *b. a decline in the sense of touch
   c. an improved sense of sight
   d. an improved sense of touch.

3. Humans are classified by biologists as belonging to the:
   a. Primate Subkingdom
   *b. Primate Order
   c. Mammalian Order
   d. Mammalian Suborder.

4. The ability to see the world in three dimensions is:
   *a. stereosocopic vision
   b. tri-scopic vision
   c. multiple vision
   d. binocular vision.

5. One of the main reasons for the constantly increasing size of the primate brain is:
   a. terrestrial existence
   b. olfactory expansion
   *c. arboreal existence
   d. aquatic adaptation.

6. In primates, the opening of the skull through which the spinal cord passes and connects to the brain has:
   a. shifted backward
   b. moved to the right
   c. grown small in size
   *d. shifted forward.

7. Studies in genetics, biochemistry, and anatomy indicate that this animal is our closest relative:
   a. gibbon
   *b. chimpanzee
   c. gorilla
   d. orangutan.

8. Group social structure among chimpanzees tends to be:
   a. rigid
   *b. rather loose
   c. vertical
   d. non-adjustable.

9. Chimpanzees frequently can be observed grooming each other. This kind of activity is similar to the human trait of:
   a. domestication of animals
   b. learning by imitation
   *c. group sociability
   d. toolmaking.

10. Toolmaking among chimpanzees is:
    *a. elementary
    b. nonexistent
    c. advanced
    d. restricted to males.

11. One of the main reasons for the great increase in size of the primate brain:
    a. temperate climate
    b. hybridization
    *c. arboreal existence
    d. warm-blood.

12. In their native haunts, the largest organizational unit among chimps is the:
    a. troop
    b. band
    c. gathering
    *d. community.

13. Ramapithecus existed about:
    a. 1 million years ago
    b. 30 million years ago
    *c. 8 to 15 million years ago
    d. 7 million years ago.

14. Australopithecus was living in Africa by:
    *a. 4 million years ago
    b. 10.5 million years ago
    c. 25 million years ago
    d. 50 million years ago.

15. Many anthropologists agree that there were basically just two kinds of Australopithecus: A. africanus and:
    a. A. australo
    b. A. proconsul
    *c. A. robustus
    d. A. leakey

16. The information-processing capacity of <u>Australopithecus</u> was about that of a modern:
    a. ten-year-old human
    *b. chimpanzee or gorilla
    c. monkey
    d. elephant.

17. Australopithecine fossils have given us proof that hominids acquired:
    *a. erect bipedal posture before their enlarged brain
    b. an enlarged brain before their erect bipedal posture
    c. body fur before hair
    d. hair before body fur.

18. Provided the bulk of <u>Australopithecus</u>' diet:
    a. fish
    b. fruit
    c. meat
    *d. vegetables.

19. The earliest identifiable tools are found in:
    *a. Ethiopia
    b. Rhodesia
    c. Australia
    d. England

20. The earliest identifiable tools are about:
    a. 500,000 years old
    *b. 2.5 million years old
    c. 4 million years old
    d. 7 million years old.

21. Provided the first clear evidence of the use of fire for protection, warmth, and cooking:
    a. Cro-Magnon
    b. Neanderthals
    *c. <u>H. erectus</u>
    d. <u>Australopithecus</u>

22. Investigations have proven that Neanderthal was:
    a. <u>H. erectus</u>
    b. Cro-Magnon
    c. <u>Australopithecus</u>
    *d. <u>H. sapiens</u>

23. There is evidence that Neanderthals:
    a. executed the disabled
    *b. cared for the disabled
    c. ignored the disabled
    d. had no disabled.

24. The toolmaking tradition of the Neanderthals is called:
   a. Devonian
   b. Oldowan
   *c. Mousterian
   d. pebble-tool.

25. There is evidence to suggest that Neanderthals:
   *a. evolved into modern humans
   b. disappeared 100,000 years ago
   c. had no magico-religious ceremonies
   d. had fewer tool types than previous traditions.

26. Cro-Magnons are classified as:
   a. Homo sapiens
   *b. Homo sapiens sapiens
   c. Homo Cro-Magnon
   d. Homo sapiens Cro-Magnonensis.

27. With the arrival of Cro-Magnon, culture became a more potent force than:
   a. predators
   b. recreation
   c. religion
   *d. biology.

28. Cultural adaptation became highly specific and regional during the:
   a. Upper Mesolithic
   *b. Upper Paleolithic
   c. Lower Paleolithic
   d. Middle Mesolithic.

29. A stone tool with chisel-like edges:
   a. atlatl
   b. Oldowan chopper
   *c. burin
   d. Mousterian ax.

30. With this invention a hunter increased the force behind a spear throw:
   *a. atlatl
   b. burin
   c. spear-springer
   d. bandolier.

Essay Questions

1. Describe the basic anatomical features common to all primates and indicate their importance in the evolutionary change of early hominids.

2. The two major predecessors of <u>Homo</u> <u>sapiens</u> were far advanced culturally over their hominid ancestors. Name these two and describe the cultural adaptations each made to assure their survival and speed evolutionary change.

CHAPTER 4: LANGUAGE AND COMMUNICATION

Multiple Choice Questions

1. Sounds or gestures that stand for meanings among a group
   of people:
   a. Hebrew script
   b. signals
   c. cosigns
   *d. symbols.

2. Washoe is remarkable in that she:
   a. is able to communicate with signs
   b. has learned how to cook
   *c. has been able to learn and use human symbols
   d. is able to imitate human sounds.

3. A gesture which has a natural or biological meaning is
   called a(n):
   a. instinct
   *b. signal
   c. symbol
   d. myth.

4. The modern scienfific study of language is known as:
   a. glottochronology
   b. kinesics
   *c. linguistics
   d. phonology.

5. _____ are sounds that make a difference in meaning.
   *a. phonemes
   b. allophones
   c. minimal pairs
   d. voice inflection

6. In linguistics, a method of dating divergence in branches
   of language families:
   *a. glottochronology
   b. diversion
   c. linguistic chronology
   d. language subgrouping.

7. The approximate maximum number of sounds used in any
   language around the world:
   a. 26
   *b. 50
   c. 100
   d. 250.

8. Different sounds belonging to the same sound class, or phoneme:
   *a. allophones
   b. minimal pairs
   c. cosigns
   d. morphemes.

9. The smallest units of sounds that carry a meaning are called:
   a. informants
   b. phonemes
   c. allophones
   *d. morphemes.

10. The _____ of a language consists of all the observations about its morphemes and its syntax.
    a. style
    b. structure
    *c. grammar
    d. frame substitutions.

11. "A system of extralinguistic noises which generally accompany language" best describes which of the following areas of study?
    a. kinesics
    *b. paralanguage
    c. descriptive linguistics
    d. ethnolinguistics.

12. Paralanguage is best described by which of the following:
    a. "One picture is worth a thousand words."
    b. "What you say is what you get."
    *c. "It's not what he said so much as how he said it."
    d. "The message is the medium."

13. The study of "body language" is called:
    *a. kinesics
    b. paralinguistics
    c. extralinguistics
    d. vocal linguistics.

14. Historical linguistics, in terms of its anthropological applications, provides a means of:
    a. working with the language of a given people
    b. speaking with the people being studied
    *c. dating certain migrations, invasions, and contacts with people
    d. deciphering living languages.

15. An example of a kinesic message in the U.S.A. would be:
    a. a man beating his breast in Tarzan fashion
    b. staggering home after a wild party
    c. blowing one's nose when infected by a cold virus
    *d. nodding one's head "yes" or shaking it "no".

16. The historical study of language investigates, at least in part:
    a. all the features of a given language
    b. only classical languages
    c. only languages which are spoken in variants in our
          period
    *d. relationships between earlier and later forms of the
          same language.

17. Which of the following does not describe a major force
    for linguistic change?
    a. borrowing
    *b. labeling
    c. linguistic nationalism
    d. phonological differences between groups of differing
          status.

18. Studies the relationships between language and culture:
    a. paralinguistics
    b. semantics
    c. transformational grammar
    *d. ethnolinguistics.

19. According to the Whorfian hypothesis:
    *a. language shapes culture
    b. life fashions language
    c. culture shapes language
    d. language and culture have a reciprocal influence.

20. Once a language terminology is established, it tends to:
    a. change at a constant rate
    b. become rigid and inflexible
    *c. perpetuate itself and to reflect the social structure
    d. become enmeshed with kinship terms that reflect the
          concerns of a group.

21. Taboo words reveal something about:
    *a. the beliefs and social relationships of a particular
          culture
    b. the universality of culture, since most words that are
          taboo in Western culture are taboo throughout the
          world
    c. the universality of fear and obsessions, since most
          cultures share these in some form
    d. the irrational prejudices of culture.

22. Code-switching in dialect studies refers to:
    a. changing from one level of language to another
    b. changing from one language to another
    c. changing from one dialect to another
    *d. all of the above.

23. Sociolinguists generally study:
    a. social dialects
    b. multilingualism
    c. the structure of folk tales and folk songs
    *d. all of the above.

24. Varying forms of a language that are similar enough to be mutually intelligible:
    a. languages
    *b. dialects
    c. boundary markers
    d. pidgin languages.

25. The ability to refer to things and events removed in time and space:
    a. transformation
    b. code switching
    *c. displacement
    d. framing.

26. According to Chomsky, the finished product, the complete utterance or sentence is said to display:
    *a. surface structure
    b. complete structure
    c. transformational structure
    d. structure.

27. The theoretical linguistic theory that attempts to find the complete set of rules capable of generating or producing all possible sentences in a language:
    a. deep structure
    b. sociolinguistic grammar
    c. glottochronology
    *d. a transformation-generative grammar.

28. A linguist who developed the first logical and consistent model for scientifically describing what happens in the whole sentence-making process:
    a. B. F. Skinner
    b. William Labov
    c. David Premack
    *d. Noam Chomsky.

29. No matter what origin or type, a language must:
   *a. work well enough for people to be able to share and
           communicate needs
    b. resist most efforts to change its basic lexicon
    c. be flexible enough to describe "snow" twenty-four
           different ways
    d. all of the above.

30. Koko the gorilla has been taught to communicate with:
     a. pictographs
    *b. American Sign Language
     c. computers
     d. typewriters

Essay Questions

1. If you were an anthropological linguist in the field
   ready to describe a previously unwritten language, what
   steps would you take in order to analyze it?

2. Does language affect culture, or is it affected by
   culture? How does the Whorfian hypothesis contribute to
   an understanding of this relationship?

CHAPTER 5: CULTURE AND PERSONALITY

Multiple Choice Questions

1. The <u>tabula rasa</u> theory propounded by Locke stated that:
    a. newborn humans inherit their personality from the
         father's side as well as from the mother's
    *b. adult personalities are exlusively the products of
         their postnatal experiences
    c. there is a basic similarity to all human personalities
    d. newborn humans do not have a personality.

2. Enculturation is the:
    a. process of transmitting society from one generation to
         the next
    b. process of transmitting social norms from one adult to
         another
    c. process of transmitting culture from one child to
         another
    *d. process of transmitting culture from one generation to
         the next.

3. Self-awareness in anthropology refers to:
    a. primarily the process of self-identification
    b. the process of adaptation of the self to the objects
         of an environment
    *c. the ability to identify oneself as an object, to react
         to oneself, and to appraise oneself
    d. the ability to determine right actions from wrong
         actions.

4. According to the author, the environment in which one
    lives must be objectified, labeled, and explained,
    because:
    a. time-space orientation varies so much from person-to-
         person and culture-to-culture that it must be
         explained
    b. the norms and objects of one's environment are usually
         very difficult to understand
    c. visuals help humans to understand more
    *d. an orderly universe seems essential as a setting for
         orderly behavior.

5. Personality is a concept used in anthropology to mean:
    a. an integrated dynamic system of perceptual assemblages
    *b. an integrated dynamic system of perceptual assemblages
         that develop over time
    c. a person's cognitive map
    d. the distinctive way a person presents himself or
         herself to others.

6. Personalities are products of enculturation:
   a. and as such are likely to change structure very
      frequently
   b. and cannot be inherited in any way
   *c. as experienced by individuals, each with a particular
      genetic makeup
   d. and are located primarily in the heart.

7. This book is generally credited as marking the beginning
   of the field of culture and personality:
   a. Growing Up in New Guinea
   *b. Coming of Age in Samoa
   c. Patterns of Culture
   d. Totem and Taboo

8. Samoan children learn they can have their way if they are
   quiet and obedient. Consequently, Samoan children grow
   up:
   *a. with minimum social stress
   b. resentful and vindictive
   c. independent
   d. dependent.

9. One of the first scholars to challenge the universality
   of the Oedipus Complex theory:
   a. Jung
   *b. Malinowski
   c. Boas
   d. Locke

10. The behavioral environment in which this group's self
    operated consisted of a flat world:
    a. Ojibwa
    b. Menominee
    *c. Penobscot
    d. Iroquois.

11. The agents of enculturation in any culture tend to be
    primarily:
    *a. the family, kinsmen, and peers
    b. only the family
    c. fellow members of one's play group or age association
    d. one's father and mother and older siblings.

12. How people feel about themselves and others:
    a. cognitive dissonance
    b. self-other awareness
    c. perceptual appraisal
    *d. patterns of affect.

13. Freud in Totem and Taboo saw the Oedipus complex as:
    a. the most important factor in group personality
       development
    *b. the most important factor in individual personality
       development
    c. the most important factor in dependence training
    d. uniquely applicable to most primitive societies.

14. Which of the following would be an example of the
    Apollonian mode of behavior as described by Benedict?
    a. a stag party
    b. a psychedelic party
    *c. Sunday service in a U.S. Christian church
    d. a religious retreat where the retreatants fast from
       food for an extended period of time.

15. This anthropologist used the terms "Dionysian" and
    "Apollonian" in her classic book, Patterns of Culture:
    a. Mead
    b. DuBois
    c. Mair
    *d. Benedict.

16. Which of the following peoples were not part of Patterns
    of Culture?
    a. Dobu
    b. Zuni
    *c. Bantu
    d. Kwakiutl.

17. Culture and personality specialists began in the 1960s to
    refer to their field as:
    *a. psychological anthropology
    b. personality and culture
    c. cultural patterning
    d. cognition and culture.

18. The principle of "share and share alike" is the "order of
    the day" in:
    a. contemporary China
    b. American society
    c. horticultural societies
    *d. hunting and gathering societies.

19. The statement that "Madmen are logical--as are the
    French" is an example of an American:
    a. national character belief
    *b. stereotype about the French
    c. view of normality
    d. view of abnormality.

20. One of the main problems of using psychological tests like the T.A.T. is:
   a. many primitive peoples cannot "read" pictures
   b. not everyone has the same personality
   *c. that tests devised in one cultural setting may not be appropriate in another
   d. some societies have little or no self-awareness.

21. The Japanese national character study by G. Gorer was important in:
   *a. pointing out the dangers of generalizing from minimal evidence to explain complex social phenomena
   b. pointing out the importance of Japanese sphincters on the Japanese national character
   c. demonstrating the validity of national character studies
   d. demonstrating the validity of the popular proverb "Wait till the peanut butter hits the fan!"

22. When the toilet-training hypothesis on the Japanese was tested after World War II, it was found that the severity of Japanese toilet training was:
   a. underestimated
   *b. a myth
   c. restricted to females
   d. a propaganda plot.

23. A major criticism of national character study has been:
   a. that it has overemphasized fieldwork
   b. that it has not given sufficient importance to child-rearing practices in the formation of adult personality
   *c. that it has not taken into account the fact that occupational and social status tends to cut across national boundaries
   d. that it has not used a more simplistic individual psychology to explain complex social phenomena.

24. The personality typical of a society as indicated by the central tendency of a defined frequency distribution:
   a. basic personality
   *b. modal personality
   c. distributional personality
   d. standardized personality.

25. "Normality" can be defined only:
   a. by anthropologists and psychologists
   *b. by the standards of a particular society
   c. after seeing the movie One Flew over the Cuckoo's Nest
   d. after understanding what morality is.

26. Insanity, from an anthropological perspective, is:
      a. a term defining a physiological ailment
    *b. a term describing the actions of people that deviate
          widely from the behavior of "normal" people
      c. how "normal" people describe themselves
      d. indefinable because of its complexity.

27. An individual who is disturbed because he or she cannot
      adequately measure up to the norms of society and yet be
      happy is termed:
    *a. neurotic
      b. psychotic
      c. schizophrenic
      d. paranoic.

28. National character studies have generally proven to be:
    *a. based on unscientific and overgeneralized data
      b. highly objective
      c. usually objective
      d. meticulous.

29. A precise image of paranoid schizophrenia:
      a. Kayak Fright
      b. Algonkian Madness
    *c. Windigo
      d. Altolo.

30. Anthropologist Francis Hsu's approach to the study of
      national character:
      a. compares cultural role models
    *b. studies the core values of a nation's culture and
          related personality traits
      c. correlates male-female behavior with cultural norms
          and ideals
      d. studies collapsed cultures of the past in order to
          discover clues about modern cultures.

Essay Questions

  1. Discuss the concept of national character. Be sure to
     indicate your knowledge of the objections to national
     character studies.

  2. Culturally induced conflicts cannot only produce
     psychosis, but can determine the form of the psychosis as
     well. Explain the meaning of this statement.

CHAPTER 6: PATTERNS OF SUBSISTENCE

Multiple Choice Questions

1. The importance of human ecological relationships is shown by the pig festivals among the Tsembaga of New Guinea, which served the purpose(s) of:
   a. providing an outlet for discontent in the community
   *b. marking the end of hostilities and reducing the strain on food supplies when pigs became too numerous
   c. bloodletting
   d. domestication.

2. Within a human ecosystem:
   a. humans are able to change their environment
   b. environments can change humans
   c. humans can manipulate environments
   *d. all of the above.

3. Serves as an illustration of the relativity of any adaptation:
   a. Down's syndrome
   b. Tay-Sachs disease
   c. measles
   *d. sickle-cell anemia.

4. The rise of the great civilizations in China, Mesopotamia, and Peru was made possible by the independent invention of irrigation agriculture. This serves to illustrate:
   a. the process of cultural preadaptation
   *b. parallel evolution
   c. the core of culture development
   d. the concept of culture area.

5. The development of similar cultural adaptations to similar environmental conditions by peoples of quite dif-ferent cultural backgrounds is called:
   a. lineal evolution
   *b. convergent evolution
   c. parallel evolution
   d. envirolution.

6. The development of similar cultural adaptations to similar environmental conditions by peoples of somewhat similar cultural backgrounds is called:
   *a. parallel evolution
   b. convergent evolution
   c. multi-lineal evolution
   d. equal-evolution.

7. A geographic region in which there existed a number of societies following similar patterns of life:
   a. zone culture
   b. culture niche
   c. regional culture
   *d. culture area.

8. The Great Basin Shoshone Indians are divided into two groups which live in different environments. The northern Shoshone are hunters of the abundant game in their region, while the western Shoshone are gatherers of the wild crops found in their region. This situation reflects:
   *a. variations in adaptation
   b. parallel inventions
   c. randomness
   d. domestication.

9. Those features of a culture that play a part in the society's way of making its living are called its:
   a. culture boundaries
   b. subsistence markers
   *c. culture core
   d. societal modes.

10. Of all the people who have ever lived,_____ percent have been hunter-gatherers.
    *a. 90
    b. 75
    c. 50
    d. 25

11. These people must accommodate their places of residence to naturally available food sources:
    a. horticulturalists
    b. agriculturalists
    *c. hunter-gatherers
    d. pastoralists.

12. Today hunters and gatherers:
    *a. are found only in remote, marginal areas
    b. make up the majority of the world's population
    c. have not existed for 10,000 years
    d. have their pick of the best environments.

13. Which of the following is incorrect?
    a. hunting is universally a male occupation
    b. too much time spent at hunting can actually be
          counterproductive
    c. in hunter-gatherer groups women typically do the
          gathering, although it is often more arduous labor
          than hunting
    *d. hunter-gatherer camps serve identical purposes for
          human and nonhuman primates.

14. Which of the following is true?
    a. hunter-gatherers constantly live on the verge of
          starvation
    b. hunter-gatherer societies are highly stratified
    *c. hunting styles and equipment may play a role in
          determining the population size and movement of
          hunter-gatherer societies
    d. almost all hunter-gatherers cultivate some crops as
          well, by leaving a group of people at the year-
          round water wells who tend the crops.

15. The immediate event that produced the human cultural
    "revolution" transforming hunter-gatherers into food
    producers was the:
    a. development of permanent settlements
    b. development of irrigation agriculture
    c. development of the plow
    *d. the domestication of plants and animals.

16. One of the significant changes that the development of
    the domestication of crops eventually had on hunter-
    gatherers was:
    *a. the establishment of permanent settlements
    b. stimulating humans to invent the stone ax
    c. the development of egalitarian society
    d. all of the above.

17. A significant factor in !Kung Bushman regulation of
    population size:
    a. herbal contraceptives
    b. birth control pills
    *c. prolonged nursing of infants
    d. male abstinence

18. A society that employs irrigation, fertilizers, and the
    plow to produce food on large plots of land is known as:
    a. horticulturist
    *b. intensive agriculturalist
    c. pastoralist
    d. hunter-gatherer.

19. The organizing units for the social order in food-producing societies after the domestication of plants and animals became:
    *a. kinship groups
    b. females
    c. males
    d. elders (usually male).

20. Gift giving is obligatory in horticultural societies because:
    *a. it ties the whole society together
    b. it helps a man become chief
    c. there will not be any pig feasts without it
    d. men are usually the hunters even in horticultural societies.

21. In horticultural societies like the Gururumba, a family's social prestige is partially based on:
    a. the amount of gifts received from kinsmen
    b. the number of children who are food producers
    *c. the productivity of its garden
    d. a successful division of labor.

22. A frequently used method of cultivation found in many horticultural societies is called:
    a. gift exchange
    b. plow agriculture
    *c. slash-and-burn
    d. irrigation.

23. The Gururumba are like the Tsembaga in that:
    a. both are pastoralists
    *b. both hold large pig feasts that help to maintain the ecological balance
    c. both have a very complex division of labor as compared to intensive agricultural societies
    d. both rely on flexibility and mobility for subsistence.

24. In moving with their herds over large territories in response to an annual weather cycle, pastoralists are being:
    a. independent
    *b. seasonally nomadic
    c. controlled by the wishes of the khans
    d. domesticated.

25. The Bakhtiari are:
    a. a horticultural society which has exploited its environment by a slash-and-burn technology
    *b. a pastoral society which revolves around two seasonal migrations in search of better grazing lands
    c. an agricultural society in Mexico that was conquered by H. Cortez
    d. a New Guinea pig-raising society.

26. The number of people who can be supported by the available resources at a given level of technology:
    *a. carrying capacity
    b. subsistence capacity
    c. social relations density
    d. distribution density.

27. Which of the following is not an animal herded by pastoralists?
    a. cattle
    b. horses
    *c. pigs
    d. camels.

28. Pastoralists are like hunter-gatherers in that:
    *a. both tend to live in areas that are marginal--that is, in areas where land is not suitable for farming
    b. both have some members of the group who remain behind to protect the camp
    c. both count on flexibility to get the game they hunt
    d. neither ever engage in horticulture.

29. Urbanization:
    a. hastened the development of egalitarian societies
    *b. rapidly increased the pace of human cultural evolution
    c. made humans more dependent on the unpredictability of the environment
    d. all of the above.

30. One effect of the urbanization process as exemplified by the Aztecs was:
    *a. the need to increase agricultural production
    b. the need to increase the number of agricultural workers
    c. the need to develop a system of writing for statistical purposes
    d. the need to find new commercial outlets for agricultural production.

Essay Questions

1. What are the reasons for hunting being a male occupation? What contributions have women made in the gathering of food in hunting and gathering societies?

2. Counter the argument that hunter-gatherer societies are "primitive" or "backwards."

CHAPTER 7: ECONOMIC SYSTEMS

Multiple Choice Questions

1. The anthropological view that the principles of market economics <u>cannot</u> be applied in the study of societies that do not exchange goods for gain:
   *a. substantivism
   b. formalism
   c. relativism
   d. exchangism.

2. Anthropologists who hold that the principles of economics are general enough to be applied usefully to all societies:
   a. substantivists
   *b. formalists
   c. relativists
   d. exchangists.

3. Which of the following is <u>not</u> one of the major productive resources that a social group must use in production of goods and services?
   *a. sex
   b. labor
   c. capital
   d. technology.

4. In any given economic system it is necessary to interpret the economic processes of a society according to that society's culturally defined demands and conventions. This is known as what kind of a perspective?
   a. substantivist
   b. formalist
   *c. cultural relativist
   d. ethnocentric.

5. In nonindustrial and nonprofit-oriented societies, cooperative work groups exist. This type of work is characterized not by "counting the hours" but by:
   a. working during one's free time willingly
   b. working with family members only
   c. slavery
   *d. good spirit and enthusiasm.

6. Which of the following is true?
   a. Cooperative work groups can be found everywhere in nonliterate, nonindustrial, and nonpecuniary societies.
   b. In every society there is some specialization of craft.
   c. Cooperative work is not necessarily voluntary
   *d. all of the above.

7. A social obligation compelling a family to distribute goods so that no one accumulates more wealth than anyone else is a(n):
   a. reciprocity
   b. exchange
   c. redistribution
   *d. leveling mechanism.

8. Among people who produce their own food, there is apt to be more in the way of:
   a. recreation
   b. religion
   c. social classes
   *d. specialization.

9. The practice of defining territories on the basis of core features is typical of:
   a. horticulturalists
   b. pastoralists
   c. urbanists
   *d. hunters and gatherers

10. The kinds of tools that a society uses are limited primarily by its members':
    *a. lifestyles
    b. intelligence
    c. wealth
    d. all of the above.

11. _____ are found in communities where property must not be allowed to threaten a more or less egalitarian social order.
    a. capitalists
    *b. leveling mechanisms
    c. perpetuating resources
    d. industrialists

12. A civil-religious hierarchy which, on a revolving basis, conbines most of the civic and ceremonial offices of a community in a hierarchical sequence with each office being occupied for one year:
   *a. cargo system
   b. Kula ring
   c. soa
   d. cooperative

13. Technological knowledge is transmitted in nonliterate societies:
   a. in sign language
   *b. orally
   c. by drawing
   d. by men only.

14. In societies with no medium of exchange (e.g., money), produce is consumed _____ by the consumer.
   a. indirectly
   b. in terms of another good
   c. entirely
   *d. directly.

15. Mode of exchange in which the giving and the receiving are specific as to the value of the goods and the time of their delivery:
   a. negative exchange
   b. positive exchange
   c. leveling
   *d. balance reciprocity.

16. Generalized reciprocity and balanced reciprocity are both positive in the sense that neither party in an exchange cares _____ about the value of the object.
   a. much
   *b. only
   c. entirely
   d. financially.

17. In non-Western societies, pure altruism in gift giving is:
   a. more common than in our own society
   *b. as rare as in our own society
   c. seen as the work of evil spirits
   d. nonexistent.

18. A system of reciprocity where neither the value of what is given is calculated nor the time of repayment specified:
   a. balanced
   b. open-ended
   *c. generalized
   d. negativistic.

19. A form of exchange in which the giver tries to get the better of the exchange:
    a. balanced
    *b. negative
    c. positive
    d. sting.

20. A form of trade that provides for the exchange of goods between groups in spite of potential barriers:
    *a. silent
    b. barter
    c. Kula
    d. simpatico.

21. A group that participates in the Kula ring:
    a. Siriono
    b. Bushmen
    c. Hawaiians
    *d. Trobrianders.

22. The Inca civilization in Peru exchanged goods by a process called:
    a. reciprocity
    *b. redistribution
    c. leveling
    d. dirct consumption.

23. The Kula ring example serves to illustrate:
    a. silent trade
    *b. a way of overcoming the dangers of negative
            reciprocity
    c. redistribution
    d. generalized reciprocity.

24. "Conspicuous consumption" occurs only in societies that produce substantial amounts of wealth distributed _____ among people.
    *a. unequally
    b. equally
    c. fairly
    d. extensively.

25. In a society where redistribution is at the base of the exchange system, a "good" chief is one who:
    a. hoards his wealth as long as possible
    b. accumulates the most wealth
    c. has the most prestige
    *d. gives his income away generously.

26. Redistribution, as a form of exchange, is organized by a:
    a. free market
    b. kinship group in an egalitarian society
   *c. central administration, as in a chiefdom or a kingdom
    d. political party with conspicuous consumption as its
          model.

27. The potlatch ceremony of the Northwest Coast Indians is
    an example of a:
    a. balanced reciprocity
    b. negative reciprocity
    c. silent trade
   *d. leveling mechanism.

28. According to the market principle, the prices of goods
    are determined only by the process of:
    a. give and take
   *b. supply and demand
    c. reciprocal relations
    d. distribution.

29. The idea of market in non-Western societies often means
    not a principle that determines the prices of goods, but
    a_____for exchanging goods and for establishing
    and maintaining friendships.
    a. method
    b. set of rules
    c. symbol
   *d. place.

30. An example of a nonindustrial type of market-place is:
    a. the New Orleans Cotton Exchange
    b. The New York Stock Exchange
   *c. a "flea market"
    d. a "potlatch".

Essay Questions

1. Describe the Kula ring of the Trobriand Islanders.

2. What is the relationship between economics, culture, and
   the world of business? How can anthropology become
   involved?

CHAPTER 8: MARRIAGE AND THE FAMILY

Multiple Choice Questions

1. An example of where groups of children are raised by paired teams of trained male and female specialists is:
   a. Nayar of India
   *b. Israeli kibbutz
   c. Dusun of Borneo
   d. Sudan dinkas.

2. An example of a human cultural universal is:
   a. the human estrus cycle
   b. hunting-gathering aspects of families
   *c. cultural rules controlling sexual relations
   d. cultural rules prohibiting exogamy.

3. The best current explanation for the almost constant sexual receptivity of the human female relates such behavior to:
   a. diet
   b. intelligence
   *c. persistent bipedal locomotion
   d. body size

4. The leading exponent of French Structuralism is:
   a. Jean-Paul Sartre
   b. Jean-Jacques Rousseau
   c. Jacques C. Penez
   *d. Claude Levi-Strauss

5. Exogamy is:
   *a. a rule limiting one to marry outside his/her group
   b. a rule limiting one to marry inside his/her group
   c. a rule that establishes category of kinsmen
   d. generally no longer observed, even by the Nayar.

6. In Freudian theory, the attraction of the daughter to the father:
   a. Vultan complex
   *b. Electra complex
   c. Oedipus complex
   d. Venus complex.

7. A truly convincing explanation of the incest taboo:
   a. relates to psychological causes
   b. relates to biological causes
   c. was advanced by Freud
   *d. has yet to be advanced.

8. In North American society, this family form has become the ideal:
   a. core
 *b. nuclear
   c. extended
   d. consanguineal.

9. Families formed on the basis of marital ties between husband and wife are known as:
   a. consanguine families
   b. core families
 *c. conjugal families
   d. levirate families.

10. Families formed on the basis of women and their brothers and the dependent offspring of the women are known as:
    a. maternal families
  *b. consanguine families
    c. sororal families
    d. affinal families.

11. Industrial and hunting-gathering societies are alike in that:
  *a. both have a nuclear family form
    b. both have an extended family form
    c. both have consanguines living together with affines
    d. all of the above.

12. Marriage to more than one wife is called:
    a. polyandry
    b. polygamy
  *c. polygyny
    d. group marriage.

13. The Nayar household group discussed in the text is an example of a(n):
    a. nuclear family
    b. conjugal family
  *c. consanguine family
    d. affinal family.

14. The most common form of marriage is_____, probably because of_____reasons.
    a. polygyny/political
  *b. monogamy/economic
    c. polygyny/sexual
    d. monogamy/political.

15. Marriage to more than one husband is called:
    *a. polyandry
    b. polygamy
    c. polygyny
    d. bigamy.

16. A marriage custom whereby a widower marries his dead wife's sister:
    *a. sororate
    b. avunculate
    c. levirate
    d. matrilate.

17. A form of marriage where the man or the woman either marries or lives with a series of partners:
    a. communal marriage
    *b. serial marriage
    c. extended-partner marriage
    d. bigamy.

18. A collection of nuclear families, related by ties of blood, that live together:
    a. serial family
    b. blood family
    c. conjugal family
    *d. extended family.

19. Divorce:
    *a. is possible in all societies
    b. does not occur in preliterate groups
    c. occurs in four of five societies
    d. occurs in seven of ten societies.

20. In the Old Testament, the marriage of Jacob's son, Onan, to his dead brother's wife is an example of:
    a. the rule of exogamy
    *b. the custom of the levirate
    c. the violation of the incest taboo
    d. polygyny.

21. The nuclear family of industrialized societies has evolved from:
    *a. the extended family form
    b. the group marriage form
    c. the serial marriage form
    d. rampant divorces.

22. The bride price is:
    a. money or goods presented to the bride by the groom
    b. a compensation to the family of the groom for his loss
   *c. a compensation to the family of the bride for their loss
    d. a compensation paid directly to the groom.

23. A period of time during which the groom works for the bride's family:
    a. groom service
   *b. bride service
    c. in-law service
    d. marital service.

24. Residence patterns seem closely related to the nature of a society's:
   *a. economy
    b. family form
    c. politics
    d. marriage type.

25. Sororal polygyny is marriage:
   *a. to women who are sisters
    b. to men who are brothers
    c. of a sister to her brother
    d. of a woman to two or more uncles.

26. The residence pattern where a woman may live with the family in which her husband grew up:
   *a. patrilocal
    b. avunculocal
    c. matrilocal
    d. extra-local.

27. The residence pattern where a married couple may live with the husband's mother's brother:
    a. matrilocal
    b. matriarchal
    c. ambilocal
   *d. avunculocal.

28. Which residence pattern is best suited for our own society?
    a. patrilocal
   *b. neolocal
    c. ambilocal
    d. avunculocal.

29. One frequently used means to handle the problem of conflict between spouses in a polygynous marriage is:
   a. through serial monogamy
   b. through frequent divorce
   c. through building separate houses in separate villages for spouses
   *d. through sororal polygyny.

30. Extended families have their own potential areas of stress. Two of these are:
   a. independence training and decision-making
   *b. decision-making and the problem of in-marrying spouses
   c. decision-making and dependence training
   d. polygyny and incest.

Essay Questions

1. The universality of the incest taboo has long interested anthropologists. Discuss the various explanations for this taboo.

2. What are the five common patterns of residence that a newly married couple may adopt? Why do different societies practice patterns of residence?

CHAPTER 9: KINSHIP AND DESCENT

Multiple Choice Questions

1. Kinship has an important place in some nonindustrial societies, because:
   *a. it is a successful basis for the political decision-making process
   b. everyone in the same tribe knows everyone else and they all trust each other to use their kinship connections wisely
   c. kinship ties are usually more important than family ties
   d. all of the above.

2. A descent group is, at bottom, nothing more than:
   a. an unstructured kin group
   b. the "glue" which holds kin groups together
   c. a voluntary association
   *d. a structured social group.

3. This descent group is the most common form in non-Western societies:
   a. bilineal
   *b. unilineal
   c. ambilateral
   d. kindred.

4. There is a close relationship between the descent system and the _____ of a society.
   a. government
   b. historical age
   *c. economy
   d. religion.

5. The Tikopia of Polynesia are a:
   *a. patrilineal society
   b. matriarchy
   c. bilateral descent society
   d. matrilineal society.

6. The founder of kinship studies is:
   a. Edward B. Tylor
   b. Alfred L. Kroeber
   *c. Lewis Henry Morgan
   d. Ruth Benedict.

7. In a patrilineal descent system which of the following would <u>not</u> be a member of ego's descent group?
  a. the daughter
  b. the sister
*c. the mother
  d. the father.

8. Which of the following is true of the Tikopia?
  a. the father's sister has ritual power and authority akin to those of her sister-in-law
  b. social status is determined by age
*c. residence is patrilocal
  d. the <u>paito</u> has no economic structure.

9. The matrilineal pattern is similar to the patrilineal one in that descent does <u>not</u> confer:
  a. inheritance rights to men
  b. power to men
*c. authority to women
  d. inheritance rights to women.

10. Which of the following is true of matrilineal systems?
*a. a father's property is inherited by his sister's sons
  b. divorce is very rare
  c. the husband has legal authority in his sister's household
  d. brother-sister bonds are weak.

11. According to the author, one serious disadvantage of a matrilineal descent system is:
  a. the lack of a strong male-oriented lineage
*b. the considerable tension that usually exists between husband and wife due to conflicting lineage loyalties
  c. the difficulty children have in identifying an authority figure
  d. the weakened brother-sister bonds that cause family tension.

12. An ambilineal system is more_____with regard to descent affiliation than is a unilineal system.
  a. structured
*b. flexible
  c. loose
  d. exclusive.

13. In this system, descent is matrilineal for some purposes and patrilineal for others:
  a. bilateral descent
*b. double descent
  c. duo-lineal descent
  d. multiple descent.

14. A descent system whereby each individual has the option of affiliating with either the mother's or the father's descent group:
    a. voluntary descent
    b. ego's choice
    c. forked merging
    *d. ambilineal.

15. A common feature of lineages is that they are:
    a. endogamous
    *b. exogamous
    c. ambilineal
    d. non-ancestor oriented.

16. A patrilineal descent group can be corporate if:
    a. the members trace descent through male links to a common ancestor
    b. the members hold sacred beliefs in common
    c. the members perform sacred (totemic) rituals in common
    *d. the members own property in common and there is generational continuity.

17. Because a descent group continues to exist after the death of members as new members are continually born into it, it is called a:
    *a. corporate group
    b. legal group
    c. post mortem group
    d. rotating kinship organization.

18. The founding ancestor of this descent group lived so far in the past that the links to the ancestor are assumed rather than known.
    a. lineage
    b. ramage
    *c. clan
    d. kindred.

19. A set of customs and beliefs by which there is set up a special system of relations between the society and certain plants, animals, and other natural objects:
    *a. totemism
    b. animism
    c. animatism
    d. ontogeny.

20. A unilineal descent group composed of two or more clans which are supposedly related:
    a. moiety
    b. clan
    c. sib
    *d. phratry.

21. This descent group exists when an entire society is divided into two and only two major descent groups:
    a. clan
    *b. moiety
    c. phratry
    d. bifocality.

22. Trobriand society is organized along strict:
    a. patrilineal lines
    b. avuncular lines
    *c. matrilineal lines
    d. ambilineal lines

23. Which of the following is a unilineal descent group in which each member assumes descent from a common ancestor but is unable to trace actual genealogical links back to the ancestor?
    a. clan
    b. phratry
    c. moiety
    *d. all of the above.

24. A group of people closely related to one living individual through both that person's parents is called:
    a. a descent group
    b. a sibling
    *c. a kindred
    d. an affinal kin group.

25. The people of the United States generally have a:
    a. patrilineal descent system
    b. ambilineal descent system
    c. matrilineal descent system
    *d. bilateral descent system.

26. A kindred is a weaker social unit than a descent group because:
    a. it cannot be turned to for economic aid
    *b. it cannot function as a group except in relation to ego
    c. it can be too easily administered
    d. ego does not know all of its members

27. Which of the following kinship systems is used by American society?
    *a. Eskimo
    b. Omaha
    c. Hawaiian
    d. Iroquois.

28. Of the different systems of kinship terminology discussed by the author, which of the following is the least complex?
    a. Eskimo
    b. Omaha
    *c. Hawaiian
    d. Crow.

29. The original Jewish descent groups in New York City are known as:
    a. Yiddish lines
    b. Chautauguas
    *c. family circles
    d. Yentas.

30. A kinship terminology system in which some of family members are separated and given different names while other kin are combined under a common name is known as:
    a. bifurcated system
    b. descriptive system
    c. generational system
    *d. bifurcate-merging system.

Essay Questions

1. Describe each of the descent groups in this chapter (lineage, clan, phratry, moiety, and the kindred). What tasks does each perform for society?

2. What can a study of kinship terms tell us about a society?

CHAPTER 10: AGE, COMMON INTEREST, AND STRATIFICATION

Multiple Choice Questions

1. Sometimes called the only universal factors in the determination of one's position in society:
   a. education and wealth
   b. wealth and power
   *c. age and sex
   d. intelligence and wealth.

2. An organized group of people with membership on the basis of age is known as an age:
   *a. grade
   b. class
   c. set
   d. grouping.

3. An example of a fairly simple, straight-forward age graded society:
   a. Yanomamo
   b. Yurok
   c. Navajo
   *d. Masai

4. A group of persons initiated into an age grade that will move through the system together:
   a. age class
   b. clique
   c. novices
   *d. age set.

5. In a number of the world's traditional societies, there may be little need for women's associations because:
   *a. opportunities for female sociability are great
   b. women are treated as equals of men
   c. women disapprove of such associations
   d. men will not allow women's associations.

6. The most varied and elaborate use of grouping by age is found in:
   *a. Africa south of the Sahara
   b. Africa north of the Sahara
   c. South America
   d. New Guinea.

7. Age groupings:
   *a. complement other forms of social organization
   b. substitute for other forms of social organization
   c. supplant other forms of social organization
   d. cancel out other forms of social organization.

8. Common-interest associations are generally:
   a. not found in most societies
   *b. found in both industrial and modernizing nations
   c. not the result of individual predilections
   d. found in hunting-gathering societies as well.

9. Which of the following is a function of age groupings?
   a. They maintain social continuity.
   b. They provide "performers" for various social roles.
   c. They assist in socialization of younger children.
   *d. All of the above are functions of age groupings.

10. It has been found that common-interest associations frequently become firmly established as:
    a. men become more aware of women's traditional roles in society
    b. a centralized government is started
    *c. the people of traditional societies become urbanized
    d. people become more interested in social complexity and less interested in kinship.

11. Common-interest associations have usually been referred to as "voluntary associations" by anthropologists, but the author feels this term would not be a good one to use because:
    *a. people don't always join associations by choice
    b. people almost never join an association voluntarily
    c. it might be confused with "volunteer army"
    d. people are often required by law to join an organization.

12. As cross-cultural research makes clear, women:
    a. do not play an important role even in their own associations
    b. do play an important role in associations of their own but not in those in which men predominate
    *c. play an important role in associations of their own, and even in associations which are predominantly male
    d. usually allow men to run even women's associations.

13. Traditionally, common-interest associations have served primarily to, in some way:
    a. run governments
    b. serve the local bureaucracy
    *c. preserve local traditions, customs, and beliefs
    d. drive out demons, witches, and other disruptive agents.

14. In areas of rapid social change, common-interest associations:
    a. ultimately prove to be a barrier to the adoption of new cultural traits that would help with group survival
    *b. increasingly assume the roles and functions formerly held by kinship and age groups
    c. increasingly are encouraged by governmental reformers
    d. generally are designed to impede or slow down the push toward urban adaptation.

15. New descent groups formed by younger generations of Jews in North America:
    a. Sons of Judah
    *b. cousins clubs
    c. New Wave Jews
    d. synagogue clubs.

16. The National Organization of Women (N.O.W.) is an example of a(n):
    a. age class
    b. sex-biased class
    *c. common-interest association
    d. a sex-based stratification system.

17. The keynote of common-interest associations in the urban world is:
    a. ambition
    *b. adaptation
    c. friendliness
    d. stratification.

18. In contrast to stratified societies, egalitarian societies:
    a. give equal access to economic resources to all individuals
    b. give equal access to economic resources to all adult males and females
    *c. give equal access to economic resources at least to all adult males
    d. do not give equal access to economic resources to all individuals.

19. In egalitarian societies, social positions are based primarily on _____, whereas in stratified societies they are primarily based on _____.
    a. sex/economic factors
    b. age/ability
    c. kinship/ability
    *d. kinship/economic factors.

20. Which of the following is <u>not</u> true of stratified societies?
   a. They have hierarchically ranked groups that maintain permanent positions.
   b. They have an over-reaching ideology that provides the rationale for the entire system.
   c. They have differential control of the sources of power relative to their ranking.
  *d. They allow individuals' social position to depend primarily on their own abilities alone.

21. Castes are strongly:
  *a. endogamous
   b. exogamous
   c. mobile
   d. egalitarian.

22. Stratified societies are divided socially into:
   a. ethnic groups
   b. plural groups
  *c. social classes
   d. castes.

23. Which of the following is <u>not</u> characteristic of a caste system?
   a. membership determined by birth
   b. membership lifelong
  *c. generally exogamous
   d. some possibility of changing castes through hypergamy.

24. Which of the following is generally <u>not</u> a contemporary symbolic indicator of social class?
  *a. school attended
   b. occupation
   c. residential location
   d. form of recreation.

25. In the United States, mobility:
   a. takes place during the early years of one's life
   b. takes place in automobiles
  *c. usually involves a move up or down of only a notch
   d. is easier than one would suppose.

26. An example of a very restrictive, closed stratification society is:
   a. U.S.S.R.
  *b. India
   c. Cuba
   d. U.S.A.

27. Mobility is:
    a. not generally present in all stratified societies
  *b. is present even in caste systems of stratification
    c. not possible in the so-called Communist countries
    d. is almost unlimited in open-class societies like the
          United States of America.

28. In societies having extended families, mobility is
    usually:
    a. easy
    b. downward
    c. prohibited
  *d. difficult.

29. At the top of the cast hierarchy in India:
  *a. Brahmins
    b. untouchables
    c. warriors
    d. landowners

30. In Tiriki each age group contains those men who were
    initiated not simply during one year, but over an age
    span of:
    a. three years
    b. five years
    c. ten years
  *d. fifteen years.

Essay Questions

  1. How are some groups of individuals in traditional
     societies trying to cope with the disruptive effects of
     modernization and urbanization on their social
     organizations? (By forming common-interest associations
     in urban areas that facilitate the individual's
     adaptation to the urban environment.) How do the
     institutions they devise operate?

  2. Describe each of the three main ways social classes are
     given expression.

CHAPTER 11: POLITICAL ORGANIZATION AND SOCIAL CONTROL

Multiple Choice Questions

1. The <u>least</u> complicated form of political organization is:
     a. tribe
     b. unit
   *c. band
     d. sect.

2. Probably the oldest form of political organization:
     a. tribe
   *b. band
     c. unit
     d. chiefdom.

3. Among the !Kung Bushmen of the Kalahari Desert, the <u>kxau</u>, or owner, has authority if he:
   *a. remains in his territory
     b. has a verbal deed
     c. has the support of the headmen
     d. has rights of inheritance.

4. An example of an uncentralized authority system:
   *a. tribe
     b. state
     c. chiefdom
     d. principality.

5. Tribal political organizations are relatively:
   *a. more like bands, except there are more people with whom to contend
     b. more like chiefdoms, except they have no chief
     c. more like states, lacking only a bureaucracy
     d. not found among pastoralists.

6. In bands, leaders become such by virtue of their:
     a. lineage
     b. heritage
     c. age
   *d. abilities

7. Political organization based upon segmentary lineages is associated with a kind of economic production in which each lineage group produces_____ goods.
     a. different
     b. useful
     c. surplus
   *d. the same.

8. The segmentary lineage system is similar in operation to the:
   *a. clan
   b. moiety
   c. phratry
   d. kindred.

9. Throughout much of Melanesia there appears a type of leader called:
   a. Prophet
   b. Great Tiki
   c. Ruling Elder
   *d. Big Man.

10. One way a leader can acquire status and power in a tribal society like that of the Kapauku of West New Guinea is by:
    a. oratorical ability
    b. obtaining a second wife
    *c. obligating people to him through loans
    d. giving many gifts.

11. The chief is the head of a:
    *a. redistributive exchange system
    b. reciprocity exchange system
    c. market exchange system
    d. leveling system.

12. A prime technique of resolving disputes at the band level:
    a. heritage
    b. religious beliefs
    *c. mobility
    d. divination

13. A chiefdom is a society stratified according to:
    *a. descent
    b. wealth
    c. intelligence
    d. physical prowess.

14. The Swazi of Swaziland are noted for their:
    a. band organization
    b. tribal organization
    c. chiefdom
    *d. state system.

15. Which of the following is only characteristic of state systems?
    a. military
    b. warrior class
    *c. police
    d. unequal ranking of members.

16. State societies are usually run by:
    a. informal decision-making groups
    b. the chief of state
    *c. a bureaucracy
    d. the military.

17. Whatever form the political organization of a society may take, and whatever else it may do, it is always involved in one way or another with:
    a. religion
    *b. social control
    c. mutual cooperation
    d. stratification.

18. A system of controls so thoroughly ingrained in each person that each becomes personally responsible for his or her own good conduct:
    a. naturalized
    b. legitimatized
    *c. internalized
    d. externalized.

19. Such incentives to conformity as awards, titles, and recognition are known as_____sanctions.
    a. titular
    *b. positive
    c. affirmative
    d. social.

20. An important pioneer in the anthropological study of law:
    a. Benedict
    b. Mead
    c. Harris
    *d. Hoebel.

21. When disputing parties settle a dispute by means of argument and compromise:
    a. disputation
    *b. negotiation
    c. agreement
    d. settlement.

22. When an unbiased third person makes an ultimate decision in an argument:
    a. arbitration
    *b. adjudication
    c. disputation
    d. umpire.

23. In a trial by ordeal, judgment is thought to be made by:
   *a. supernatural powers
   b. luck
   c. unbiased natural process
   d. political intrigue.

24. There is reason to suppose that war has become a serious problem only in the last:
   a. 10 years
   b. 40 years
   c. 2,000 years
   *d. 10,000 years.

25. Warfare is most prominent among which of these populations?
   a. hunting and gathering
   *b. farming and pastoral
   c. island
   d. herders.

26. This world view is an important prerequisite to inter-societal warfare among food-producing peoples:
   a. naturalistic
   b. combatative
   *c. exploitative
   d. organic.

27. Almost invariably, peaceful societies are those that have some form of_____world view.
   *a. naturalistic
   b. organic
   c. Christian
   d. exploitative

28. These political systems are marked by an increased reliance upon coercion as a means of social control:
   a. uncentralized
   *b. centralized
   c. disparate
   d. Western.

29. Basic to the political process is the concept of:
   *a. legitimacy
   b. force
   c. wealth
   d. fairness.

30. In Western societies, offenses against individuals are called:
    a. crimes
    b. arguments
    c. illegal altercations
    *d. torts.

Essay Questions

1. What is the difference between a Big Man type leader in tribal organization and a chief in a chiefdom? Give examples to illustrate your answer.

2. What are some of the suggested causes of the existence of warfare in human societies? Why would a rise in population density be a cause of warfare? Is there any relationship between world view and the frequency of the occurrence of warfare?

CHAPTER 12: RELIGION AND MAGIC

Multiple Choice Questions

1. Anthropologists study religious beliefs in order to:
   a. prove the existence of a supreme being
   b. search for the metaphysical truth of human existence
   *c. show how each religion embodies a number of "truths" about humans and society
   d. show that science can answer most questions about the present "unknown".

2. A minimal definition of religion true in all human societies would be: "Religion is a belief in the existence of:
   *a. supernatural beings or powers"
   b. major deities"
   c. ancestral spirits"
   d. good and evil."

3. A belief in supernatural beings presupposes:
   a. that humans create the images of them in their own likeness
   *b. that the supernatural beings have an interest in human affairs
   c. that all individuals turn to prayer in their time of need
   d. the existence of witchcraft as well.

4. Strong beliefs in ancestral spirits are frequently found in societies that:
   a. are hunter-gatherers
   b. are food-producers
   c. are pastoralists
   *d. have strong descent-based groups.

5. A belief in personal spirits which are thought to give life to nature is called:
   *a. animism
   b. religion
   c. animatism
   d. pantheonism.

6. A common, though not invariable, feature of pantheons is:
   a. a vengeful supreme being that created the world or universe
   b. a supreme being that is feared by the people
   c. a benevolent supreme being
   *d. the existence of a supreme being, even though people may not pay much attention to it.

7. Conceived the concept of animism:
   *a. Sir Edward Tylor
   b. Bronislaw Malinowski
   c. Lewis Henry Morgan
   d. Sir Thomas Jeans.

8. Anthropologists use the Melanesian term _mana_ to refer to:
   a. animistic beliefs
   *b. a belief in an impersonal supernatural power
   c. a belief in ancestral spirits
   d. a belief in nature spirits.

9. A term used in the United States that is nearly equivalent to the meaning of animatism is:
   a. "freakie"
   b. "myth"
   *c. a belief in ancestral spirits
   d. a belief in nature spirits.

10. Priest (or priestess) is to shaman as:
    a. natural power is to supernatural power
    b. ceremony is to ritual
    c. religion is to witchcraft
    *d. group presentation is to individual representation.

11. Which of the following is an example of the difference between a priest and a shaman?
    a. shamans are always males, while sex is not important for the priesthood
    b. only priests are involved in formal, ritualistic ceremonies
    c. priests are generally only ceremonialists, while shamans have the power to communicate with the deities and spirits
    *d. priests tell the people what to do and shamans tell the supernaturals what to do.

12. Shamans regard their ability to perform "tricks" for their clients as:
    a. probably unethical, and they generally realize it
    b. a worthwile enterprise because they get higher fees
    c. probably an excess but generally accepted and recognized as necessary by the clients
    *d. proof of their superior powers.

13. Rituals which pertain to stages in the life cycle of the individual are known as:
    *a. rites of passage
    b. rites of intensification
    c. sorcery
    d. rites of transition.

14. Rituals that take place during crises in the life of the group are known as:
     a. rites of passage
    *b. rites of intensification
     c. sorcery
     d. rites of transition

15. A funeral is an example of:
     a. a rite of passage
     b. a rite of intensification
     c. "religion in action"
    *d. all of the above.

16. Which of the following is correct?
    *a. Magic is more like science than it is religion, according to Frazer.
     b. Westerners are no longer fascinated by the existence of notions about magic
     c. Magical practices are primarily characteristic of small-scale, food-producing societies
     d. all of the above.

17. The performance of ritual:
     a. has little or no meaning in industrial societies
     b. is carried out mostly in nonindustrial societies
    *c. does not have to be limited to times of overt crisis
     d. can easily help to increase the anxiety and fear of the participants.

18. Many magical incantations require the use of fingernail clippings of the chosen victim to ensure the success of the sorcery. This is an example of what kind of principle of magic?
     a. Sympathetic magic
    *b. contagious magic
     c. witch magic
     d. nightmare magic.

19. A people's beliefs about witchcraft:
     a. arise from a fear of the unknown
    *b. reflect that society's conception of evil
     c. have little or no benefit for the society
     d. are usually unfounded, as there is no such thing as a witch.

20. The belief that supernatural powers can be compelled to act in certain ways for good or evil purposes by recourse to specified formulas is known as:
     a. ritual
     b. sorcery
     c. witchcraft
    *d. magic.

21. Everyday witches are often:
    a. the social deviants of a group
    b. thought to be dangerous when offended, because they
          will retaliate with sickness, death, etc.
    c. morose, arrogant, and unfriendly
  *d. all of the above.

22. Frazer's two kinds of magic are called:
    a. empathetic and infectious
  *b. sympathetic and contagious
    c. apathetic and sorcery
    d. witchcraft and sorcery.

23. Among the Azande, deliberate actions undertaken for the
    purpose of doing specific harm are:
    a. wizardry
    b. witchery
  *c. sorcery
    d. all of the above.

24. One function of witchcraft is to:
    a. prevent hostile feelings from being released and
          disrupting the society
  *b. provide another means of social control
    c. make people feel more in control of their daily lives
    d. counteract the pervasive control of religion over the
          daily lives of the people of a society.

25. When the unknown is explained and made understandable,
    the fears and anxieties of individuals are reduced. This
    is an example of a:
    a. social function of religion
    b. social function of witchcraft
  *c. psychological function of religion
    d. psychological function of witchcraft

26. A totemic ritual is an example of the:
  *a. social function of religion
    b. basic uniformity of all religions
    c. psychological function of religion
    d. way religious beliefs can lead to certain social and
          cultural excesses.

27. Which of the following persons could we say led a
    revitalization movement?
    a. Geronimo
  *b. Jesus Christ
    c. John F. Kennedy
    d. "Che" Guevara.

28. Revitalization movements provide an example of religion's:
   a. conservative strength
   *b. revolutionary potential
   c. failure to provide a totally encompassing world view
   d. steady deterioration in modern, industrial societies.

29. Cargo cults are really:
   a. religious substitutes
   b. anti-religious
   *c. religiously oriented solutions for Melanesian natives to obtain social and economic relief
   d. religious movements oriented towards preaching the doctrine that the rewards of humans will come in heaven.

30. Anthropologist Anthony Wallace holds that all religions stem from:
   a. fear
   b. ancient Egypt
   c. animatism
   *d. revitalization movements.

Essay Questions

1. What is the difference between magic and witchcraft?

2. Describe revitalization movements and give an example from contemporary or recent United States history. Explain whether your example was successful or not and the reasons why.

CHAPTER 13: THE ARTS

Multiple Choice Questions

1. Art, like language, is:
   a. dependent
   *b. symbolic
   c. the same from society-to-society
   d. all of the above.

2. Noting that art is a common feature of all cultures, some writers have suggested that:
   a. the artist was the most important member of his/her group
   b. all cultures derive from one source
   *c. humans have a need or drive for art
   d. all humans share the same ideas.

3. There appears to be no culture in the world without at least some art form, even if it is only in the form of:
   a. sculpture
   b. craft objects
   *c. storytelling or rudimentary kinds of singing or dancing
   d. a rudimentary drum.

4. Art in human societies is usually:
   a. not a luxury
   b. a necessary kind of social behavior
   c. engaged in by all active human beings
   *d. all of the above.

5. The academic discipline that studies folklore, concentrates on folk tales, and works on cross-cultural comparisons of themes, motifs, and structures, is called:
   *a. folklore
   b. literary anthropology
   c. legendology
   d. semantics.

6. Of the verbal arts, the narrative has received the most attention and study because:
   a. it is very popular
   *b. it is very popular in our own (U.S.A.) culture
   c. it is a dying art form and people wish to record it before it is gone
   d. it lends itself well to analysis.

7. One of the easiest kinds of verbal arts to record or collect is:
   a. poetry
   b. drama
   c. insults
   *d. narrative.

8. The study of narratives is divided into three major categories, which are:
   a. myth, epic, and tale
   b. myth, legend, and motif
   c. tale, legend, and motif
   *d. myth, legend, and tale.

9. The prime function of a myth is:
   a. to make people question the fundamental values of their cultures
   b. to provide entertainment, since every culture needs some way to break up the monotony of routine
   c. to produce social solidarity
   *d. to depict and describe an orderly universe.

10. In myths, people try to:
    *a. answer ultimate questions
    b. amuse themselves
    c. communicate news
    d. worship deities.

11. It may be said that myth is the_____of cultures which do not verify "truth" about nature by means of experiment.
    *a. science
    b. religion
    c. magic
    d. superstition.

12. One of the dangers and problems of myth interpretation is:
    a. that not everyone in a society observes the morals of the myth
    b. that not everyone may have heard the myth
    *c. that not everyone may accept the myth or even understand it in the same way
    d. that specialists in interpreting myths may not be available to the anthropologist.

13. Epics are typically found in:
    a. all cultures
    b. the most primitive cultures
    c. tribal societies ruled by patriarchs
    *d. nonliterate societies having complex political organization.

14. Legends are most important for what they tell about:
    a. the people's reasoning powers
    *b. the ethics of the community
    c. the community's history
    d. the vocabulary of the people.

15. The study of myths is important to ethnologists because they:
    *a. express and reveal, in part, a people's world view
    b. show how myths originally spread out from one early
            myth
    c. explain people's behavior
    d. explain what kinds of religious beliefs people usually
            practice.

16. The narrative brought to television, called The Lone Ranger, is a:
    a. myth
    *b. legend
    c. tale
    d. world view.

17. The myth is basically:
    a. artistic
    *b. religious
    c. anti-religious
    d. a child's story.

18. Semi-historical narratives that account for the deeds of heroes, the movements of peoples, and the establishment of local customs:
    a. myths
    b. tales
    *c. legends
    d. incantations.

19. A creative narrative recognized as fiction for entertainment:
    *a. tales
    b. legends
    c. incantations
    d. epic.

20. Evidence for either cultural contacts or cultural isolation is provided in:
    a. myths
    b. legends
    c. music
    *d. tales.

21. The Western system of tones is called:
    a. pentatonic
    b. natural
    *c. semitonal
    d. octaval.

22. The study of music in specific cultural settings is:
    a. regional musicology
    b. culturomusicology
    c. the geography of music
    *d. ethnomusicology

23. In music, scale systems and their modifications:
    a. counterpoint
    *b. tonality
    c. semitones
    d. homophonics.

24. One reason all cultures value music is:
    *a. it is a creative skill to be proud of
    b. it has magical properties
    c. it can only be understood by those of the same culture
    d. it is closely related to art.

25. A repetition of phrases in songs has the main function of:
    *a. giving symbolic form
    b. giving emphasis
    c. adding emphasis to trivia
    d. making songs more easily remembered.

26. Sculpture differs from other skillfully created objects in that:
    a. craft objects last longer
    b. sculpture is never practical
    c. craft objects are more symbolic
    *d. sculpture is expressly produced as sculpture.

27. Plastic art is a more modern term for:
    a. abstract painting
    *b. sculpture
    c. changing art styles
    d. Renaissance wall painting.

28. The widest variety of expression in African sculpture is found in the:
    *a. ritual mask
    b. Benin bronzes
    c. pottery of Liberia
    d. dolls of Ashanti.

29. The majority of West African sculpture is:
    a. representational
    b. ritualistic
    c. nonsymbolic
   *d. abstract.

30. Ritual masks in West Africa are:
    a. still rather poor as compared to other areas of Africa
    b. usually representational
    c. nonabstract
   *d. often themselves an expression of world view.

Essay Questions:

1. Describe the three basic categories of narratives: myth, legend, and tale.

2. What are the functions of music? Why is music universal?

CHAPTER 14: CULTURE CHANGE

Multiple Choice Questions

1. Chance discoveries of new principles are:
    *a. primary innovations
    b. secondary innovations
    c. independent innovations
    d. happenstance innovations

2. The discovery that the firing of clay makes the material
    permanently hard is a(n):
    *a. primary innovation
    b. secondary innovation
    c. independent innovation
    d. happenstance innovation

3. Which of the following is a major cause of culture
    change?
    a. adaptation to changes in the environment
    b. individual variations in the way people within a
        culture view its characteristics
    c. contact with other groups
    *d. all of the above.

4. The telephone in the United States is an example of:
    *a. innovation
    b. diffusion
    c. cultural loss
    d. acculturation.

5. Culture change:
    *a. may be slow or rapid
    b. usually occurs only in "advanced" state systems
    c. is not readily apparent in the evolution of cultures
    d. is seldom good for a culture.

6. One common cause of culture change is:
    a. genetic mutation
    *b. change in environment
    c. conjunctions of celestial bodies
    d. individual initiative.

7. An innovation will probably be accepted as long as:
    *a. it is reasonably consistent with a society's needs,
        values, and goals.
    b. it does not compete with the item it replaces
    c. the inventor has little or no prestige among the
        people
    d. it is somewhat impractical and nonthreatening to the
        established technology.

8. Diffusion is:
   a. an infrequent occurrence
   *b. very commonplace
   c. found in only a few societies
   d. a relatively recent concept in anthropology.

9. Cited in the text as one reason why the United States continues to reject the metric system:
   a. cost
   *b. ethnocentrism
   c. inability to understand the system
   d. lack of practical use

10. Cultural borrowing:
    a. substitution
    b. incorporation
    *c. diffusion
    d. syncretism.

11. Linton suggested that borrowing accounts for _____ percent of any culture's content.
    a. 25
    b. 50
    c. 75
    *d. 90

12. If one looks very closely at the definition of modernization, one sees that "becoming modern" really means:
    *a. "becoming more like us"
    b. technologically equal
    c. entering the computer world
    d. "stamping out savagery".

13. Borrowing is most likely to take place in which of the following areas:
    *a. technology
    b. religion
    c. art
    d. kinship.

14. The abandonment of a cultural trait or practice without replacement:
    a. negative trait
    *b. cultural loss
    c. cultural imbalance
    d. trait attrition.

15. An example of a recent American revitalization movement:
    a. health studies
    *b. Moral Majority
    c. conservative politics
    d. separation of church and state.

16. When one culture loses autonomy but retains its identity as a subculture after acculturation has taken place, that culture has become:
    a. adapted
    b. assimilated
    c. extinct
    *d. incorporated.

17. This mechanism of change always involves an element of force:
    *a. acculturation
    b. diffusion
    c. innovation
    d. cultural loss

18. The presence of a "slave culture" in United States plantations in the early 1800s is an example of:
    a. invention
    b. diffusion
    c. cultural loss
    *d. acculturation.

19. The blending of old traits to form a new system:
    a. substitution
    b. ethnomic
    c. cultural addition
    *d. syncretism.

20. Occurs when two cultures lose their separate identities and form a single culture:
    a. adaptation
    b. synthesis
    c. symbiosis
    *d. merger or fusion

21. These innovations are improvements made by applying known principles:
    a. capital
    b. primary
    *c. secondary
    d. tertiary.

22. This anthropologist was instrumental in liberalizing immigration policies in the United States:
    a. Alfred Kroeber
    b. Ruth Benedict
    *c. Franz Boas
    d. Margaret Mead.

23. The absence of boats among the inhabitants of the Canary Islands is an example of:
    a. stimulus loss
    b. assimilative nonreplacement
    *c. loss without replacement
    d. negative diffusion.

24. If a culture's values get widely out of step with reality, this may develop:
    a. slavery
    b. caste system
    *c. revitalization movement
    d. modernization.

25. Which of the following is <u>not</u> a part of the modernization process?
    *a. population growth
    b. technological development
    c. agricultural development
    d. urbanization.

26. An attempt to resurrect a suppressed pariah group that has long suffered in an inferior social standing and has its own special subcultural ideology is known as:
    a. a revivalistic movement
    b. cargo cult
    c. a transitional group movement
    *d. a millenarian movement.

27. The movement among today's youth in the United States to establish a new set of values and life-styles in opposition to the dominant values of our culture is a striking example of:
    a. millenarism
    *b. revitalization
    c. political revolution
    d. primary invention.

28. An example of strength and resiliency in the face of European domination may be seen in the Trobriand Islander's adoption of:
    a. hockey
    b. polo
    c. baseball
    *d. cricket.

29. These Ecuadorian Indians modernized in order to escape the destruction that has occurred among many other Amazonian tribes:
    a. Siriono
    b. Yanomamo
   *c. Shuar
    d. Jivaro.

30. The use of snowmobiles among the Skolt Lapps:
   *a. had dire consequences for their pastoral way of life
    b. made reindeer herding more efficient
    c. had the unintended effect of making the Lapps more independent than before, even though the government had wanted to incorporate them into the country more effectively
    d. provides a good example of forced change.

Essay Questions

1. Why has applied anthropology historically been associated with colonialism?

2. Discuss the modernization process. Must it always be painful? Why is it sometimes quite painful?

CHAPTER 15: THE FUTURE OF HUMANITY

Multiple Choice Questions

1. Humans may be moving toward a "one-world culture." This is because of:
   a. the Westernization of other countries
   b. rapid developments in trade
   c. the exchange of scholars, students, soldiers, and others between countries
   *d. all of the above.

2. If one looks back over the past 5,000 years of human history, one will see that there has been a clear trend for political units to become larger and more all-encompassing, while at the same time they are:
   a. more bureaucratic
   b. more extensive in number
   *c. fewer in number
   d. less corrupt.

3. The social and political interaction within the same society of people with different ways of living and thinking is known as:
   a. ethnocentrism
   *b. cultural pluralism
   c. one-world culture
   d. environmental protection.

4. Which of the following anthropologists wrote, ". . . although culture is 'for' man, it is also 'against' him"?
   a. Marvin Harris
   *b. Jules Henry
   c. Margaret Mead
   d. Solon Kimball.

5. Haviland is concerned about some of the world's people declaring other whole societies:
   *a. obsolete
   b. unworthy
   c. warmongers
   d. distrustful

6. The 1985 Union Carbide accident in India which killed 2,000 people and injured at least 200,000 more, is an example of:
   a. Western hostility
   b. global retaliation
   *c. structural violence
   d. global apartheid

7. It seems that in the United States, a true cultural pluralism is:
   a. finally decreasing
   *b. finally emerging
   c. being held constant, with little or no further differentiation of subcultural groups being recognized
   d. nonexistent.

8. Cultural pluralism presently is:
   a. not supported by anthropologists
   *b. found throughout the world
   c. a step backward with regard to the achievement of global equilibrium and peace
   d. not found in African societies that have strong tribal backgrounds.

9. In order for cultural pluralism to be successfully adapted in countries with different cultural groups:
   *a. ethnocentric beliefs must be eliminated or modified
   b. ethnocentric beliefs must be strengthened or modified
   c. ethnocentrism must replace the trend toward a "one-world culture"
   d. the process of Westernization should be accelerated before a nuclear holocaust takes place.

10. Ethnocentrism usually:
    a. has no positive function in human societies
    b. is the natural result of cultural pluralism
    *c. has several positive functions in human societies
    d. is found only in industrialized societies.

11. When birth and death rates are in equilibrium:
    a. population balance
    b. demographic equalization
    c. birth control
    *d. replacement reproduction.

12. Social and political interaction within the same society of people with different ways of thinking:
    a. structural reciprocity
    *b. cultural pluralism
    c. ethnocentrism
    d. holistic differentiation.

13. A major problem associated with cultural pluralism:
    *a. ethnocentrism
    b. wealth
    c. poverty
    d. environment.

14. It is difficult to make pluralism work when cultural traditions are:
    a. new
    b. very old
    c. similar
    *d. divergent

15. Anthropologist Melville Herskovits believed that any culture that institutionalizes ethnocentrism is basing its policy on psychocultural:
    a. mysticism
    b. singleness
    c. acculturation
    *d. unreality.

16. Regarding modernization, there seems to be a strengthening tendency for people all around the world to:
    a. accept its inevitability
    b. move eagerly toward it
    c. deny its existence
    *d. resist and retreat from it.

17. Which of the following has <u>not</u> affected population growth?
    a. increased longevity
    *b. urbanization
    c. advances in medicine
    d. improved agricultural techniques.

18. The U.S. Congress passed anti-apartheid legislation in:
    a. 1917
    b. 1945
    c. 1973
    *d. 1985.

19. This country may be about the only country where pluralism has really worked out:
    *a. Switzerland
    b. Botswana
    c. Falkland Islands
    d. New Guinea

20. Anthropologists can help to resolve the problem of bringing more land into agricultural production by:
a. convincing large landholders to redistribute their land among landless peasants
b. convincing peasants to pool their land resources to make way for more efficient, large-scale productive enterprises
*c. making policy makers and planners aware of long-forgotten systems of agricultural production
d. all of the above.

21. According to Haviland, which of the following is a major problem of the future that anthropologists can have a hand in helping to solve?
a. warfare
b. schizophrenia
*c. food shortages
d. declining birth rates.

22. Discussed at some length in Chapter 15 as an example of a pluralistic society:
a. Venezuela
b. New Guinea
c. Greenland
*d. Guatemala.

23. Recommendations for changes in people's tastes and customs, which may be necessary for their survival, may involve anthropologists in:
a. economic problems
*b. ethical problems
c. positive ethnocentrism
d. United Nations.

24. The more _____ cultural traditions are, the more difficult it appears to make pluralism work.
a. similar
b. democratic
*c. divergent
d. conservative.

25. Regarding food resources, the immediate problem is not so much one of overpopulation as it is:
a. food production
*b. food distribution
c. technology
d. communication.

26. Apartheid consists of programs or measures that aim at the maintenance of:
    a. religious persecution
    b. low birth rates
    c. high literacy rates
   *d. racial segregation.

27. Violence exerted by situation, institutions, and social-political, and economic structures:
   *a. structural
    b. global
    c. peripheral
    d. secondary.

28. Meeting the problems of structural violence today probably only can be done if we are able to:
    a. increase law and order legislation
   *b. reduce the birth rate
    c. eliminate poverty
    d. enforce existing laws.

29. Its introduction in parts of India proved to be a more effective means of birth control than the devices and information offered by the government:
    a. hydropower
    b. automobile
   *c. electricity
    d. sewing machine.

30. Which of the following is <u>incorrect</u>?
    a. In some societies, the number of children an individual has is a sign of prestige.
    b. Minorities often view birth control programs as subtle plots by the majority to diminish their numbers.
    c. Most of the world's unfarmed land is marginal.
   *d. In the Middle East, motherhood and fatherhood are frowned upon as undesirable institutions.

Essay Questions

1. Discuss some of the problems associated with the rise of multinational corporations.

2. Discuss some of the flaws frequently seen in future-oriented literature.

CHAPTER 16: THE FUTURE OF ANTHROPOLOGY

Multiple Choice Questions

1. The deliberate extermination of ethnic groups:
   a. homicide
   b. planned ethnicide
   *c. genocide
   d. holocaust.

2. An organization of anthropologists in the United States explicitly concerned with the human rights and survival of indigenous cultures the world over:
   a. S.A.V.E.
   *b. Cultural Survival, Inc.
   c. A.N.T.H.R.O.
   d. Anthropological Resource Center.

3. Bill Holm, an anthropologist, played a key role in the Canadian government's decision in 1951 to drop the ban on:
   a. Indian education
   b. termination of reservations
   *c. potlatching
   d. Indian-white marriages.

4. One reason many developing countries dislike Westerners coming in and studying them is because these countries:
   *a. were once colonies of the West
   b. are upset with modern world politics
   c. think UNESCO is a joke
   d. disapprove of so-called "anthropological studies."

5. Sometimes anthropologists have difficulty in studying modernizing countries because:
   *a. people in some of them do not like to be observed as if they were strange creatures in a glass cage
   b. anthropologists have not been trained to work in modern countries
   c. anthropologists are unfamiliar with sociology
   d. anthropologists do not ask permission to do research, which is unethical.

6. In the 1950s, large amounts of research money allowed anthropologists to do research_____ as never before.
   a. on American cities
   b. at a purely abstract level
   c. at European and Asian universities
   *d. abroad.

7. An anthropologist who made a speciality of studying North
   American culture:
   a. Allan Holmberg
   *b. Jules Henry
   c. David Andrews
   d. Rosalind Sackoff.

8. A major reason social scientists have been frustrated in
   their efforts to study ways of life in the United States:
   a. little financial support from the government
   b. closeness causes research bias
   *c. the large number of separate subcultures
   d. poor image of social scientists by the general public.

9. Some of the greatest health problems in North America do
   not have to do with medical knowledge and capabilities,
   but with:
   *a. health care delivery
   b. poverty
   c. antagonism towards doctors
   d. environmental problems.

10. In community-based psychiatry, psychiatrists collaborate
    with:
    a. traditional psychiatrists
    b. non-traditional psychiatrists
    c. community leaders
    *d. traditional leaders.

11. Most anthropologists are presently employed in:
    a. government
    b. international business
    *c. colleges and universities
    d. international development agencies.

12. The great English pioneer in anthropology, Sir Edward B.
    Tylor, viewed anthropology as a:
    a. "junkyard of social sciences"
    *b. "reformer's science"
    c. "futile science"
    d. "magnificent obsession."

13. During the 1930s, there was a strong trend to the
    _____ of anthropological knowledge.
    *a. practical application
    b. Europeanization
    c. abstraction
    d. simplification.

14. After World War II, anthropologists were almost exclusively concerned with:
    a. American Indians
   *b. teaching and research
    c. practical application of anthropology
    d. New Guinea, Africa, and South America.

15. Presently, more and more anthropologists are:
    a. teaching in colleges and universities
    b. doing basic research
   *c. taking jobs outside of academic institutions
    d. becoming sociologists.

16. Over the past decade there has been in anthropology a hot debate over the subject of:
    a. academic pay
   *b. ethics
    c. training and education of anthropologists
    d. archeological methods.

17. Ruth Benedict's The Crysanthemum and the Sword (1946) was an analysis of Japanese:
    a. religious attitudes
   *b. national character
    c. athletics
    d. archeology.

18. Caused anthropologists in the United States to reexamine the ethics of their ties to government:
   *a. Project Camelot
    b. the Great Depression
    c. Project Ropewalk
    d. Selective Service System.

19. The Original Study at the end of this chapter looks at the careers of three anthropologists, all of whom:
    a. teach at colleges and universities
    b. are employed by the government
   *c. work outside of the traditional academic setting
    d. specialize in the anthropology of American cities.

20. Archeologists have an ethical responsibility to:
    a. continue their research everywhere
   *b. not sell or take the artifacts they find outside of
          the country where they are working
    c. dig up every known archeological site
    d. prevent past cultures from being forgotten.

21. Archeological research that has a practical value (e.g., archeologists serving as consultants to law enforcement agencies):
    a. legal archeology
    b. action archeology
    c. relevant archeology
    *d. applied archeology

22. The United States for many years failed to implement a 1970 UNESCO convention that would severely limit:
    a. an exchange program for anthropologists
    b. archeological excavation in foreign countries
    c. traffic in narcotics
    *d. traffic in antiquities.

23. In the 1960s,_____ publicized the fact that there were important anthropological problems to be dealt with at home as well as abroad.
    a. U.S. Senate
    *b. civil rights movements
    c. Alpha Pi Delta
    d. Turhon Murad.

24. There is currently a new and fruitful area of cooperation between anthropology and:
    a. physical education
    b. business management
    c. political science
    *d. sociology.

25. Jules Henry felt that the American anthropologist faces a flood of information coming from:
    *a. printing presses
    b. fellow anthropologists
    c. television
    d. movies.

26. Although anthropologists have studied such things as midwestern hamlets and Appalachian religious cults, many of their recent studies in the United States fall under the heading of:
    a. historical anthropology
    *b. urban anthropology
    c. Eastern American anthropology
    d. metropolitan anthropology.

27. Lewis Henry Morgan applied his anthropological knowledge by:
    a. intensive self-analysis
    b. organizing a medical union
    *c. assisting the Seneca Indians
    d. participating in Indian ceremonies.

28. Some anthropologists have worked for the Indians themselves, rather than the government, especially in connection with:
*a. Indian Land Claims
b. Indian ceremonies
c. traditional Indian religions
d. helping Indians rediscover original hunting
      techniques.

29. An international competition open to all projects, programs, or activities which illustrate the translation of anthropological knowledge into action:
a. Kroeber Prize
*b. Praxis Award
c. Guggenheim Fellowship
d. Wenner-Gren Scholarship

30. In 1982, this organization issued a policy requiring that the rights and autonomy of tribal peoples and minorities must be guaranteed in any development project (in which the organization was involved):
a. Greenpeace
b. Reformed Quaker Church
c. AID
*d. World Bank.

Essay Questions

1. In recent years more and more U.S. anthropologists have become involved in studies of their own culture. Why is this, and what are some of the problems encountered by the anthropologist conducting such research?

2. The kinds of research and job opportunities in which anthropologists are now involved raises a number of important questions concerning anthropological ethics. Discuss these ethical problems.